Extreme Savings: The #1 Guide To Getting Anything You Want For Free with Extreme
Couponing 101 Secrets, Proven Ways To Save Money, and Financial Fitness
by The Editors of SmartBuddy Books
Copyright ©2013

Extreme Savings may be ordered through booksellers or by visiting
www.ExtremeSavingsBook.com

The views expressed in this work are sole those of the author and do not
necessarily reflect the views of the publisher, and the publisher hereby disclaims
any responsibility for them.

Table of Contents

Save Money and Win Fun Prizes!
1. Go To: www.CouponCodeWorld.com
2. Click on "PriceMatch Game".
3. Enter Code: extremesavings850

Introduction:

Thank you for choosing to invest in *Extreme Savings*.

This book will indeed pay for itself FAST!

The opening topic is *Extreme Couponing 101*. You will learn the same tips and strategies used by die-hard couponers to score incredible deals on groceries. You will learn why those little coupons in the Sunday newspaper should be considered money. In fact, coupons are actually treated as a method of payment just like cash or charge at the store register.

According to NCH marketing over 332 billion coupons are redeemed annually putting $3.7 billion dollars back into pockets of consumers. The average couponing family saves $1,000 per year.

That's money in the bank!

Have you ever wondered how some people walk out of store with a bunch of stuff for FREE without stealing it?

You will soon be able to answer that question and actually DO IT yourself after you read *Extreme Couponing 101*. Yes, you will be LEGALLY stealing quite a few items soon. After *Extreme Couponing 101*, we'll move on to *How To Save Money Everyday* where you'll learn some tips on how to save money on practically anything even without coupons.

There are so many narrow-minded books on the market that solely focus on coupons as the only way to save money. Unfortunately, many people are left with impression they absolutely will not get a great deal without coupons. You can save money with or without coupons. *Extreme Savings* will show you how to do it both ways.

We'll wrap up everything with *Financial Fitness Blueprint*, which provides tips on how to improve your credit report, eliminate debt, and reach your financial goals. The key to achieving wealth is saving your money. *Extreme Savings* is going to put you on a path toward true financial prosperity so you can **LIVE FREE!**

There is much information to absorb. Take your time navigating through each section. Enjoy the ride!

Why I Use Coupons
By Darcy Stevens (CouponCodeWorld.com Contributor)

I grab a random coupon I find and go to the store, eager to save money. And then I realize that $0.25 off of the name brand product is still more than the generic.

What a load of rubbish! My sister-in-law was into couponing and occasionally told me about some great deals she got, sometimes sharing some of her cheap or free goodies with me. She offered to teach me how…but I still remembered my disappointment last time I tried to use a coupon. Maybe some day….

Enter stage right: Prince Charming. I met my husband and after getting hitched, I decided to get proactive about finances. Knowing that a major cause of marital problems is financial problems, I wanted to nip it in the bud! With a few thousand dollars of debt from my schooling and him starting his schooling, we knew we were going to be low on cash. It was perfect timing when a local class was offered at our church about couponing, and I will now never go back!

Learning to pair sales and store rewards with coupons and rebates can be difficult for some, and many people tell me that they just don't have the time for it. I don't think I could ever go back to that mentality. Here are a few reasons why couponing, and frugality in general have become a way of life for me:

The Game: I honestly didn't expect saving money to give such a rush, to be a fun game to see how low you can get your bill while getting tons of stuff for pocket change. But it is. My husband is even in on it. I still remember the first time we did a huge grocery haul and his face went from fear to elation when the total lowered by more than half.

Living Better: I've heard the phrase "Live like no one else now so you can live like no one else later". We scrimp and save now so that our future can be beautiful. Debt is a nasty four letter word and we are determined to get rid of it.

Last year we saved up enough money to throw an extra thousand toward my student debt without blinking and we have yet to take out student loans for my husband's schooling. Even after my husband is out of school and making a nice salary, we intend to be frugal and save up for a healthy down payment on our first home.

Doing Good: Many people are in my position-financially struggling. Some, on the other hand, don't give a thought to their pocketbook because they have a healthy income. Some of the best feelings in life come from selfless acts we perform and helping others, and coupons give me that outlet.

One time, for example, we went to a local pet shop. Their coupon policy allows a combination of a Buy 1, Get 1 Free sale with a Buy 1, Get 1 Free manufacturer coupon-essentially making everything free, you only pay taxes. We got several of these coupons from the Sunday paper from friends and family and took most of the stock the store had. We don't have a dog. But the humane society will be enjoying those gifts for a while.

Recently we went to a local drug store (I never shopped drug stores until I really learned to shop smart) and bought 8 packages of baby food and water. We also don't have children. Between my store card discount and 1 printed coupon from the internet, and store rewards offered, we paid out of pocket just over $9 and got back $12 in store rewards to use on milk or anything else we want. We made money. And what I can do is put it in a grocery bag and place it near my mailbox for the postal food drive.

Making money and doing good? Anyone not interested in that is just downright crazy!

I mentioned earlier how some people just don't have the time or can't understand couponing or sales shopping. You don't have to spend 20 hours a week studying weekly store ads or dumpster dive for coupon inserts from the newspaper to find great deals.

Find a blog or 2 that you like that shares recommendations on current deals and they'll tell you exactly what stores have what sales and where to find coupons to stretch your dollar the most. Enjoy it, invest in your present and future, and make the biggest impact you can-no matter what your budget! – *Darcy Stevens*

Extreme Couponing 101

Lets start with the definition of Extreme Couponing. Extreme Couponing is basically the practice of using coupons, store sales, and in store discount programs to save large amounts of money and accumulate stockpiles of free items.

Often the goal is to save at least 80% on the total sales checkout at the grocery store cash.

How can you do it?

In reality the majority of coupon users won't consistently save 80% on their grocery bill. Most shoppers save about 10% - 20% off with coupons, which is ok. If you accomplish that moderate range of savings you will do just fine.

However, Extreme Couponers frequently leave grocery store with shopping carts filled with food they got for free or pennies on the dollar. This book will discuss tactics used by Extreme Couponers to score incredible deals. You might consider some of the tactics as humorous, clever, or even outrageous. Extreme Couponers are known to dumpster dive for coupons.

Someone is probably in a dumpster right now looking for extra coupon inserts. Yeah, go ahead and laugh.

Unfortunately, there have been many instances when Extreme Couponers stoop to ridicules acts of desperation. A few crazy people steal newspapers from front yards. This book by no means endorses every strategy discussed. You should only use methods you feel comfortable practicing.

Also, please remember "Any discount you get at the supermarket REGARDLESS of the dollar figure is going to have a positive impact on your household finances." You'll find out exactly why later in the *Financial Fitness Blueprint* section.

Just relax and keep reading.

It all starts with ORGANIZATION

The key to effectively saving money is to first establish a system to keep your coupons and ad inserts organized. That statement may sound like common sense. But, it has to be discussed for sake of the sheer number of people reading this book who don't have a system in place. So if you have not been keeping track of your coupons the first step is to get everything in order.

Do you have a coupon organizer?

If YES, splendid.

If NO, Get one asap.

A coupon organizer is the centerpiece of the system you want to establish. It will save you time and money. Both equally important!

You can get a decent coupon organizer already assembled online. Click on "Coupon Organizers" at CouponCodeWorld.com.

Alternatively, you could make your own coupon organizer. Look for the following materials at nearest office supply store:

*Three Ring Binder
*9 Pocket Transparent Baseball Holder Style Sheets
*Avery Big Tab Two-Pocket Insertable Plastic Dividers

Simply designate spots for coupon inserts (SmartSource, Redplum, P&G Saver, etc) and weekly ad circulars. Once your coupon organizer is intact you'll be ready to hurt the supermarket!

Everything immediately goes inside the coupon organizer!

Don't allow coupon inserts to languish inside Sunday newspaper. Take them out right away. Otherwise they will probably get tossed in trash along with the newspaper.

Remember to date each insert.

The publication date is usually printed itty-bitty on side of coupon insert. It's hard to see that small print. Use a bold highlighter to write date on front of coupon inserts as illustrated in the picture.

You must keep track of the insert dates for coupon match up purposes.

How to build your coupon inventory

Now that you have coupon organizer set, the next step is to load that baby with coupons.

Extreme Couponers use different strategies or so called secrets to save big money at grocery store. But, they all share one thing in common…they always have lots and lots of coupons. If you want to save $500.00 on groceries you will need to get your hands on $500.00 worth of coupons. But, you won't find that many coupons in a typical Sunday paper.

The first place to go looking for additional coupons is on the Internet. It's arguably the best source for coupons mainly because web coupons are FREE and you can print them instantly at home.

Manufacturers are rapidly shifting their coupons from traditional print to the Internet anyway. So there is no better time for you to join the online coupon revolution.

CouponCodeWorld.com is a website you can use to locate and print coupons for your favorite products. Simply visit www.CouponCodeWorld.com and click on "View all grocery coupons in your area" to access FREE money saving grocery coupons. All you have to do is click and print the coupons you want. These coupons will go right in your coupon organizer.

Many stores including Walmart will accept online coupons, as they would with any coupon found in a Sunday newspaper. The only difference is that you didn't pay to get those coupons.

Here are other sites for printable coupons: coupons.com, smartsource.com, and valessis.com

Chase after more coupons

Some couponing blogs fail to provide links to all coupons available for their coupon match ups. They frequently send readers to one specific coupon website.

Let's say there is a wonderful deal on Kellogg's cereal. It's on sale for $1.09. The blogger may only give you one embedded link pointing to $1.00 off coupon. Well other coupon websites might have additional coupons available for Kellogg's cereal.

So if you print 2 coupons at each of the other sites, you would have 6 extra $1.00 off coupons for cereal. Here's how the transaction will look on paper:

Kellogg's Cereal
Sale Price: $6.53 ($1.09 x 6)
(-) $2.00 (Kelloggs.com Online Coupon)
(-) $2.00 (Redplum Online Coupon)
(-) $2.00 (SmartSource Online Coupon)
Total Amount Due: $0.53

In the above example, you pay only 53 cents for 6 boxes of cereal. It's easy to replicate this example. Just remember to print multiple coupons from various coupon websites rather than one site.

CouponCodeWorld.com has several coupon links. To obtain more coupons, visit each and every coupon website listed.

Get coupons directly from your favorite companies.

Most consumer product companies love to hear from shoppers who buy their products. They will reward you with money-saving coupons if you drop them an email or letter saying: "I really enjoy using your product. I would appreciate if you could send me some coupons. Thank You". That's all it takes to get FREE coupons for products that you actually enjoy using. Have you ever contacted the maker of the detergent you use to wash clothes? If the answer is NO, you probably missed out on a nice freebie. They might send you anywhere from a couple of coupons to several high value coupons you can use to get FREE products.

A common complaint about coupons is that there are so many for junk or things a person will never buy. But, these are coupons for products you use everyday. So get in touch with companies right away. You can contact your favorite brands via email to request coupons. Enter the "Brand Name" and keyword "Contact Us" in the search box at CouponCodeWorld.com to request coupons. For example if you want Welch's juice coupons, search "Welch's" and keyword "Contact Us". After your coupons arrive, place them in your coupon organizer for safe keeping until the product goes on sale at the supermarket.

In-store Coupons

Most grocery stores provide coupon dispensers on store shelves, freezer doors, and display end caps. Put a few extra coupons in your coupon organizer. Also, you may be able to download or print special in-store coupons. Visit your favorite store's website. Look for "online" or "digital" coupons link. Did you know that stores reward people who use a coupon with more coupons? Yes, these coupons are commonly referred to as "Catalinas". You might use a coupon on Kellogg's cereal and notice another coupon print out for 50 cents off Kellogg's cereal. That's a "Catalina" and you can stash it in your coupon organizer for use later. They print out at the register when you buy select items. You might get a Catalina redeemable for a freebie or discount on your next store purchase.

The Catalinas will add up fast for Extreme Savings!

Coupon Forums

You can get FREE coupons by joining online couponing groups, which are places where people actively swap coupons. Post the coupons you are seeking to trade and wait for responses. Someone will likely accept your offer. These forums tell you where to get the latest free coupons as well.

Facebook / Twitter

A growing number of leading brands now use social media to offer coupons and free samples. They will give you extra coupons and freebies in return for the opportunity to establish a relationship with you. Type your favorite products into the little search box at Facebook.com or Twitter.com. For example, if you enter keyword "Purex", the Purex page will show up in search results. Purex frequently posts printable coupons on their wall. If you want Purex coupons, click the "like" button on Purex's page.

Make a list of the products you have in your pantry and cabinets. Follow those brands on your list. You will eventually get coupons and deals for the things you really desire.

Free Mobile Coupons

Several apps have recently rolled out that allow shoppers to save money by simply using their Smartphone without ever clipping coupons. When you're ready to redeem these digital coupons, you just touch a few buttons on your phone screen and the coupon discounts will automatically be applied to your account.

Here are some services that will send free digital coupons directly to your mobile phone:

Cellfire
www.cellfire.com

Yowza
www.getyowza.com

CardStar
www.cardstar.com

13

How to Stack Digital Coupons

You could not only save money but make money when you stack digital coupons on top of other coupons.

Let's say that Sargento shredded cheese is on sale for $1.99 at local supermarket. Nancy, our smart savvy shopper has the following coupons:

(1) $1.00 off Sargento Cheese Manufacturer's Coupons.
(Nancy printed these coupons online at CouponCodeWorld.com)

(1) $1.00 off Sargento Cheese In-store Coupon)
(Nancy printed this coupon online at the supermarket's website)

The above coupons allow Nancy to leave the supermarket with one free bag of Sargento shredded cheese, which is wonderful.

However, Nancy is not quite done hurting that supermarket.

She notices the following deals on her Smartphone:

Ibotta App - Earn 75 cents cashback with purchase of any Sargento Cheese product.

SavingsStar App - Earn $1.00 cashback with purchase of any Sargento Cheese product.

So Nancy will actually leave the store with free cheese and extra $1.76 in her pocket. Here's how the transaction will look:

Sargento Shredded Cheese
Sale Price: $1.99
(-) $1.00 Manufactures Coupon
(-) $1.00 In-Store Coupon
(-) $0.75 Ibotta cash back
(-) $1.00 SavingsStar cash back

Total: $1.76 Profit

As you see in the above example when Ibotta and SavingsStar apps were combined (stacked) with other coupons the end result was a nice profit earned at checkout.

Download Ibotta and SavingsStar at CouponCodeWorld.com. Use both of those apps along with paper and printable coupons to maximize your savings.

Paid Sources For Coupons

The prior section discussed free ways to obtain coupons such as online sources, contacting manufactures directly, in-store coupons, social media, apps, etc. You would be in good shape if you merely use those free methods to acquire coupons.

However, you can bolster your coupon inventory faster if you utilize paid sources for coupons as well. The next strategies might require you to spend a little money. But you will get back whatever amount of money you invest and more in the form of savings.

Sunday Newspapers

Manufacturers issue over 332 billion coupons each year and 88% originate from those shiny inserts known as *SmartSource* and *Redplum* inside Sunday Newspapers.

Eventually coupons will only be available online. But, right now that Sunday Newspaper is still the prime source for coupons. It's also a relatively inexpensive source for savings. Think about it. The Sunday Newspaper usually has about $150.00 worth of money-saving coupons inside. So you will get a nice $150.00 return on the few bucks you spent on that newspaper.

What sounds even BETTER?

How about an extra $1,500 or $3,000 to spend at your local grocery store? You can accomplish this by doing one simple thing...LIFT MORE THAN ONE NEWSPAPER FROM THE STAND!

The typical consumer is content with only buying one Sunday newspaper at a convenience store. If there are maybe one or two coupons inside redeemable for a free item, that's considered wonderful. Let's say our savvy shopper Sherry notices a coupon redeemable for one free Dr.Pepper soda inside a Sunday newspaper insert. Sherry will head over to store and leave with one Dr.Pepper and think...WOW I got a FREE Dr.Pepper!

But, if Sherry purchased 10 newspapers, she would walk out of the store with 10 FREE Dr.Pepper sodas instead of one resulting in a much bigger WOW!

By purchasing additional newspapers, you multiply your coupon savings. Simply pull out the inserts and separate your coupons into sets for each product.

For example, you buy 10 newspapers and there is a coupon for $1.00 off Hunts ketchup in each paper. That's a sweet deal because ketchup is something that typically goes fast. You would clip the Hunts coupons and place them in your coupon organizer. When Hunts goes on sale for $1.00, you'll get 10 FREE bottles of ketchup. You could replicate this with several other items. Buy 3-10 extra Sunday newspapers each week.

If you want to save money off your subscription, click the "Discount Newspapers" link at CouponCodeWorld.com.

Extreme Couponers sometimes get free newspapers from hotels, beauty salons, car dealerships, and other business establishments. You might want to visit businesses and offer to take their old Sunday newspapers. They don't want to deal with those newspapers anyway. You are doing them a favor.

Also, ask friends and family for their unwanted newspaper coupon inserts. Post a "send me your coupon inserts" message on Facebook or Twitter.

Note: You will accumulate newspapers. So visit www.paperretiver.com to find out where you can dispose of newspapers for recycling.

Entertainment Book Coupons

Get an Entertainment Book ASAP!

Entertainment Book is a discount book with hundreds of FREE meal coupons, 2-for-1, 50% off, and other coupon discounts for local restaurants and retailers. Many people believe sites such as Groupon, which allows you to buy a voucher for half off is the best thing since sliced bread. Groupon is indeed an innovative option for consumers. But, honestly Entertainment Book is ten times better than Groupon. Each book has up to $20,000 or more in money saving coupons, yet Entertainment Book only cost around $35.00. A Groupon will cost you about $10 and you might save $10 bucks on one meal.

Just do the math...$35 for over $20,000 in savings at hundreds of places or $10 for $10 in savings at one restaurant, think about it!

You can print Entertainment Book coupons online for more savings. To receive a special discounted price, click on Entertainment Book at www.CouponCodeWorld.com. Also, you can get the Entertainment Book for as little as $8.00 if you buy it during late summer. They always mark down their books to clear inventory for next year's edition. Order extra copies of Entertainment Book for Extreme Savings!

Coupon Clipping Services

Many Extreme Couponers use online coupon-clipping services to take the work out of gathering coupons. You can choose whatever coupons you want. The service will mail you coupons already clipped and sorted. For example, let's say that Sobe bottled drinks are on sale for $1.00 and you want to stockpile Sobe. You could visit the coupon-clipping service website and order twenty $1.00 off coupons for Sobe. Take the coupons over to the supermarket and you'll leave with twenty FREE bottles of Sobe drinks.

You might see an Extreme Couponer on tv with heaps of coupons getting free groceries. However, the tv producers hardly ever disclose that the Extreme Couponer paid money to acquire those coupons from a coupon clipping service. Be careful if you are going to you use coupon-clipping services. The coupon-clipping services are in business to make a profit. Sometimes they overcharge for coupons. Never pay more than 15% of the total value of the coupons. For example, if a coupon-clipping service offers 200 coupons each for $1.00 off a product that means the coupons have a total value of $200.00. So the most you would pay is $30.00 (15% x $200.00 value).

Also, the coupon-clipping services know when you can get a free item or overage. So prices will rise accordingly. You should actually order coupons for an item when it is not on sale. You will always pay less for coupons that way. Stash the coupons in your coupon organizer and use them when there is sale going on at your local supermarket.

Here are some leading coupon-clipping services:

Coupons by Dede
www.couponsthingsbydede.com

The Coupon Clippers
www.thecouponclippers.com

The Coupon Carry-Out
www.couponcarryout.com

Be sure to compare prices for coupons. You can search for more coupon-clipping services at CouponCodeWorld.

eBay Coupons

Did you know you could get coupons on eBay?

Yes, you can actually buy extra coupons on eBay. Simply enter product name and keyword "coupon" into the search box at eBay.com. Any available coupons will display in the search results. You can order coupons in bundles of 10 or 20 to maximize your savings. For example, if you frequently buy spaghetti sauce, you could search for "Ragu Coupons" and maybe order a bundle of 20 coupons for $2.00. When Ragu goes on sale at the supermarket you'll have 20 coupons that you can use toward 20 bottles of Ragu. You will have enough spaghetti sauce to last for a very long time!

Some people don't like paying for coupons on eBay, but the idea of spending $2.00 to acquire $20 or $30 dollar in savings actually makes perfect sense. But, if you are going to buy coupons on eBay read the sellers feedback. The sellers with higher feedback ratings are more reliable. Always read the coupon description, terms, expiration date, and delivery terms. You want to allow yourself enough time to use the coupons. The seller should specify when they ship coupons.

Try buying multiple coupons from the same seller and ask the seller to combine shipping.

Also, look for coupons on items that you frequently buy. For example, you will eventually buy more bath tissue paper. So if you search for "Scott Bath Tissue Coupons" on eBay, you'll find someone selling 10 coupons for maybe $1.00 off Scott Bath Tissue. You can expect to pay about $1.99 for those 10 coupons.

You simply wait for a sale on Scott Bath Tissue. When it's on sale buy 10 packages. You will have locked in your savings. You won't have to buy bath tissue again for quite a while!

Look out for fraudulent coupons. Most coupons on eBay are legitimate, but if you do get a fake one ask for a refund and immediately report the seller to eBay.

Magazine Coupons

You can find coupons in popular magazines including Good Housekeeping, Ladies Home Journal, Family Circle, All You Magazine, and People. These publications are packed with coupons every month. Browse through various magazines at your local supermarket. If you see a hot coupon inside purchase multiple copies. Also, if you use Facebook or Twitter, post a message asking friends, neighbors, and coworkers if you can have their old magazines.

Restaurant Coupon Booklets

Several major restaurant chains sell coupon books loaded with coupons for FREE menu items. McDonalds offers a coupon book (in February, October, and December) that you can buy for just $1.00. You get 10 FREE items in each book. Buy multiple coupon booklets whenever possible. If you purchase 10 of the coupon books, you get 100 FREE McDonald's items (hamburgers, juice, milk, apple dippers...) all for ten bucks. The coupons don't expire for a while so you'll have time to gradually get your freebies at McDonalds. Remember to SHARE!

Many leading restaurant chains including Burger King, Subway, Hardees, and White Castle offer coupon books during the year. Ask your favorite restaurant if they offer a coupon book. They might give you one free of charge.

How to save money with Store Loyalty Programs

Several retailers will reward you with extra savings when you sign-up for a FREE store loyalty card. You can swipe the card at checkout. The coupon discounts are deducted from your card.

You probably have been asked several times, do you have a "you know what card"? You swipe your loyalty card in anticipation of an extra discount. It's nice to see the total amount due steadily drop on that cash register screen. But, believe it or not many people for whatever reason don't bring their loyalty card to the store. Have you ever had someone next to you at the grocery store say "Can I use your card?" and then say "Thanks, I guess you got a few more points ha ha". Well, that's a gain for you and loss for them! The loyalty cards are absolutely free, very simple to use, and result in considerable savings so there is no excuse for a person not to bring that card along when shopping. You can pop it right on your key chain for easy usage.

The cash register will often print out extra coupons for people who do use their loyalty card.

Here are some leading loyalty card programs:

Shop Your Way Rewards

The Shop Your Way Rewards program allows you to earn 10 points for every dollar you spend on purchases at Kmart stores. The points are converted into cash savings on a Shop Your Way Rewards card. It's FREE money. Lets say you have 75,000 points on your card. The check out bill is $83.00. You can ask the cashier to deduct the 75,000 points on your card (worth $75.00) from the total amount due. In this scenario, the cashier would discount $75.00 bringing your total amount due down to only $8.00. The person behind you will perhaps ask you something like "How did you do that?". Just tell the person to get a Shop Your Way Rewards card.

The prior example assumed 75,000 points, which may sound like a huge number. But, Kmart makes it easy to accumulate points fast. For example, if you opt-in to receive emails they will double or triple you points on certain purchases. So you might get 30 points for every dollar spent on groceries versus 10 points. They may give you 25,000 points for transferring a prescription.

Also, you might get Kmart coupons after swiping a Shop Your Way Rewards card at the register. These coupons are sometimes redeemable for FREE items. To learn more about the Shop Your Way Rewards program, visit: www.shopyourwayrewards.com

Target REDcard

Target REDcard is apart of Target's overall loyalty program. It works like a universal coupon that instantly will give you 5% discount off anything you buy in-store at Target or online at Target.com. That's on top of any existing sale or clearance price!

The REDcard is ideal if you really are not into clipping coupons, but want extra savings when you shop at Target. Sometimes the REDcard discount will exceed the value of newspaper coupons. You'll save money on the things you need to buy.

If you do use coupons on groceries at Target, you'll save extra with the REDcard. You have to apply for a REDCard credit card. Target offers a free debit card version of the REDCard whereas you don't have to go through an in-depth credit approval process.

It's linked to your checking account and works like a regular debit card. You'll still get the same 5% off deal with REDCard debit card as you would with the REDCard credit card. To sign up for Target REDCard, visit your local Target store and ask for an application.

CVS/Pharmacy ExtraCare

CVS/Pharmacy's ExtraCare loyalty card will allow you to get FREE items and exclusive discounts at CVS/Pharmacy. With the ExtraCare card you can earn ExtraBuck certificates when you buy certain everyday items such as toothpaste, beauty products, milk, cereal, otc medications, etc. ExtraBucks are coupons redeemable toward a future purchase. They might range in value anywhere from 50 cents to over $25.00.

Let's take a look at an ExtraBucks example:

CVS/Pharmacy advertised special:

Oral-B Pulsar Toothbrush
Sale Price: $6.00
ExtraBucks: $3.00

Crest Pro-Health Rinse
Sale Price: $4.50
ExtraBucks: $2.50

Colgate MaxFresh Toothpaste
Sale Price: $2.79
ExtraBucks: $2.00

Dean's Milk
Sale Price: $2.99
ExtraBucks: $1.00

Excedrin Extra Strength
Sale Price: 99 Cents
ExtraBucks: 99 Cents

All Laundry Detergent
Sale Price: $3.99
ExtraBucks: $2.00

Total: $21.26 - $11.49 (ExtraBucks) = $9.97

So as you can see the ExtraBucks resulted in bringing the total from $21.26 to $9.97, which is savings of over 45% off. That's not bad. But where are the freebies?

Let's see how coupons make everything cheaper when stacked with ExtraBuck savings:

CVS/Pharmacy advertised special with coupons:

Oral-B Pulsar Toothbrush
Sale Price: $6.00
ExtraBucks: $3.00
Manufacturer Coupon: $3.00

Crest Pro-Health Rinse
Sale Price: $4.50
ExtraBucks: $2.50
Manufacturer Coupon: $2.00

Colgate MaxFresh Toothpaste
Sale Price: $2.79
ExtraBucks: $2.00
Manufacturer Coupon: 75 Cents

Dean's Milk
Sale Price: $2.99
ExtraBucks: $1.00
Manufacturer Coupon: 50 Cents

Excedrin Extra Strength
Sale Price: 99 Cents
ExtraBucks: 99 Cents
Manufacturer Coupon: $1.00

All Laundry Detergent
Sale Price: $3.99
ExtraBucks: $2.00
Manufacturer Coupon: $2.00

Total: $21.26 - $11.49 (ExtraBucks) = $9.97 – $9.25 (Coupons) = 72 Cents. WOW!

When you match coupons with ExtraBucks in the above example, you get several items for FREE. You get toothpaste, milk, and detergent all for only **72 cents.** This is how coupon pros work their magic at CVS/Pharmacy. The above example only mentioned a few items. You will typically be able to get several items essentially for FREE each week with your CVS/Pharmacy ExtraCare card.

Check the CVS/Pharmacy circular in Sunday newspaper. The weekly CVS/Pharmacy circular specifies what items are FREE with ExtraCare card.

 There is an ExtraCare kiosk at the front of every CVS/Pharmacy that will dispense unadvertised coupons when you insert your ExtraCare card. Many people ignore that machine and walk pass it. But, you might be very surprised at what comes out of that machine. So try it out next time you visit CVS/Pharmacy.

It's almost as if CVS/Pharmacy is paying you to shop in their stores. But of course the true goal is to reel you into CVS/Pharmacy with expectations that you will buy items not on sale. They want you to spend more money than you anticipated.

Micro Shopping

You will beat the impulse to over spend by *Micro Shopping*, which is the practice of buying a small list of items that will cost the exact value of the ExtraBucks you expect to receive at checkout.

Let's say you buy the following items at CVS/Pharmacy:

Zyrtec
Sale Price: $5.99
ExtraBucks: $5.99

Bayer Aspirin
Sale Price: $3.00
ExtraBucks: $3.00

You know this transaction is going to produce $8.99 in ExtraBucks. CVS would prefer that you use the $8.99 in ExtraBucks toward a purchase that will far exceed $8.99 and maybe spend an additional $50.00 on impulse items, which have better profit margins. But, you'll come out ahead if you stick to a *Micro Shopping* list similar to the following:

Dozen Eggs
Sale Price: $1.49

Orbit Gum
Sale Price: 99 cents

Wonder Bread
Sale Price: $1.49

Purex Detergent
Sales Price: $3.99
Manufacturer Coupon: $1.00

Duracell Batteries
Sale Price: $2.49

Sub Total: $10.45 - $1.00 (Coupon) = $9.45 (Amount Due - $8.99 ExtraBucks) = 46 cents, YES!

So in this example the amount due $9.45 is close to the $8.99 in ExtraBucks. You don't see $50.00 worth of items, which is what CVS wanted to happen.

The $8.99 in ExtraBucks allowed shopper to get one dozen eggs, chewing gum, bread, detergent, and batteries all for just **46 cents**!

This is what you want to accomplish with ExtraBucks.

CVS/Pharmacy Couponing Tips:

CVS/Pharmacy will send you valuable in-store coupons if you provide your email address on ExtraCare Card sign-up form.

You need an ExtraCare Card to receive advertised sale prices in the weekly circular.

CVS/Pharmacy ExtraBucks are only valid on future purchases. You can't apply ExtraBucks to same transaction that produced Reward.

Not all ExtraBucks deals will be gems. If you see something like Claritin priced for $16.99 with a $1.00 ExtraBuck, but you don't use Claritin then don't buy it. It's not free after the ExtraBucks and you don't use it so don't buy it. This might sound obvious to the average person. But, so many people buy things just because it's advertised as ExtraBucks items.

A product could actually be priced lower elsewhere even with the ExtraBucks. That same box of Claritin might be on sale at Walmart for $10.99. You have to pay close attention to the price of ExtraBucks items. Make sure you are really getting the best deal.

Sometimes there is a limit on the number of items you can purchase to earn ExtraBucks. If the promo states a limit of two (2) ExtraBucks, you should buy two items so you can get two (2) free ExtraBucks. But if it clearly says limit of one (1) ExtraBuck, you will only get one (1) ExtraBuck. Remember to read the fine print for the item when you are looking through the CVS/Pharmacy ad. It will specify any ExtraBuck purchase limits.

Supermarket Loyalty Cards

Practically every leading supermarket offers some type of customer loyalty program whereas they will give you a free loyalty card, which allows you to save additional money at checkout on top of coupon savings. The loyalty card is not a big secret and you probably use one when you shop. But, what so many people overlook is the fact that the entire loyalty program may go far and beyond what they expect. If you don't take 100% full advantage of a store loyalty program you will miss out on real savings.

Here's an example of fully utilizing Kroger's loyalty program one of the most popular nationwide.

Diana's Kroger Checkout Receipt:

Deans Milk (1-Gallon)
Reg Price: $2.79
Kroger Plus Card Savings: $1.29
Manufacturer Coupon: $0.50

Fresh Bakery Dinner Rolls
Reg Price: $4.00
Kroger Plus Card Savings: $0.35

New York Strip Steak
Reg Price: $8.50
Kroger Plus Card Savings: $2.35

Market Deli Sliced Cheese
Reg Price: $7.50
Kroger Plus Card Savings: $1.50

Kashi Cereal (8 boxes)
Reg Price: $41.65
(-) Manufacturer Coupon: $5.00
(-) Kroger Plus Card Savings: $2.00
(-) Kroger 123 Reward Savings: $25.00
(-) Kroger R/X Reward Savings: $25.00

Total Amount Due: $1.49

WOW, WAIT A MINUTE!

Are you thinking how was it possible for Diana to get premium steak, fresh bakery bread, deli cheese, and eight boxes of cereal all for **ONLY $1.49?**

Well, on this particular day Diana used a $25.00 bonus she got for transferring a prescription (their was a coupon in the paper). Also, she got another $25.00 off with her Kroger 123 MasterCard, which is apart of Kroger's overall loyalty program. All of these little perks brought her total down to just $1.49.

There are so many money-saving benefits available from Kroger's loyalty program. The same likely rings true for the loyalty program of the supermarket you normally shop at as well. You need to take full advantage of the loyalty program. Find out if you can get bonus rewards when you sign up for store branded Visa or MasterCard. Ask the pharmacy if they have any deals going whereas you get store credit for transferring your prescription.

Visit the customer service desk at your favorite supermarket and request brochure that explains their loyalty program. You should squeeze each and every red cent out of it.

Walgreen Balance Rewards

Walgreens Balance Rewards works similar to other loyalty programs. You earn in-store coupons (Register Rewards) when you buy certain items. Here are a few actual Walgreens Register Rewards promotions from the past:

Sobe Lifewater
Sale Price: 99 Cents
REGISTER REWARDS: 99 Cents
(Good on Next Purchase)

Omega Smart Fish Oils
Sale Price: $10.00
REGISTER REWARDS: $10.00

Healthy Women Soy Supplement
Sale Price: $10.00
REGISTER REWARDS: $10.00

Total: $20.99 - $20.99 (Register Rewards) = FREE

So if you bought all three of the above items you would have $20.99 in Register Rewards to use on a future purchase. If you were going to spend twenty bucks at Walgreens anyway it would make perfect sense to buy those items. Also, you'll notice that when the Register Rewards equal the total amount due as in the above example, you are getting the items for FREE.

You can often profit from Walgreens Register Rewards.

Let's take a look at those items again this time matched with manufacturer coupons.

SoBe Lifewater
Sale Price: 99 Cents
REGISTER REWARDS: 99 Cents
Manufacturer Coupon: $1.00

Omega Smart Fish Oils
Sale Price: $10.00
Manufacturer Coupon: $5.00
REGISTER REWARDS: $10.00

Healthy Women Soy Supplement
Sale Price: $8.00
Manufacturer Coupon: $5.00
REGISTER REWARDS: $8.00

Total: $20.99 - $20.99 (RR) - $11.00 (Coupons)
= $11.00 Profit

You should attempt to match manufacturer coupons with Register Rewards savings to maximize your savings at Walgreens.

Other things to remember about Register Rewards:

You can find Register Reward deals in Walgreens ad insert.

Walgreens Register Rewards are only valid on future purchases. So you can't apply the Register Rewards to same transaction that produced the Reward.

You can't use multiple Register Reward coupons on a single item, which is frustrating to people who have several Register Reward coupons, and just want to use them toward one item.

For example, if you have 20 Register Reward coupons, you must buy at least 20 items not just a single item.

But, you could add 19 pieces of cheap candy or other inexpensive items to meet that restriction.

Walgreens Couponing Tips:

Walgreens offers a separate coupon book called Walgreens Savings Book at the front of store with coupons and rebates not in the regular ad insert. You can combine coupons in this book with manufacturer coupons and in-store savings. For example, Quaker Oatmeal is on sale for $1.99 and there is a $1.00 off coupon in the Walgreens Savings Book. You have another $1.00 manufacturer coupon for Quaker Oatmeal. Here's how your savings would look:

Quaker Oatmeal: $1.99 (Sale Price)
- $1.00 Off Walgreen Coupon
- $1.00 Off Manufacturer Coupon = FREE Oatmeal

So don't ignore that coupon book located next to the ad inserts. It's the key to Extreme Savings at Walgreens.

You can get additional coupons at Walgreens.com

How to play the coupon matching game

Once you have your coupon inventory together, the next step is to find out when and where to match coupons with items on sale.

Thanks to migration of weekly sales ads to the Internet, you can instantly see what is on sale at your local store. The vast majority of stores have their entire weekly sales ad readily available online. Each week you should browse various supermarket sites. The goal is to match coupons in your coupon organizer with items on sale in the ad. You can actually memorize the coupons in your coupon organizer if you look through it 2-3 times a week. A mental alert in your head will sound off when an item in the ad matches a coupon in your organizer. It's almost like playing one of those kid memory games.

You glance over the ads looking for items that match your coupons. When you see a matching item make note of it. After you are done looking at the ads, go through your list of matching items and pull out the corresponding coupons. It's then just a matter of taking your matched coupons over to the store.

To view online store ads, click on "Weekly Store Ads" at www.CouponCodeWorld.com

Use CouponMom

CouponMom is a leading couponing forum started by coupon extraordinaire Stephanie Nelson. It's a FREE online resource that will help you easily match coupons in your coupon organizer with items on sale (including unadvertised specials) at your local grocery store. For example, if Colgate toothpaste is on sale for $1.00 at your local supermarket, and there is a $1.00 coupon for Colgate toothpaste out there CouponMom will tell you the exact date of the insert that has the $1.00 coupon.

All you have to do is grab that dated insert from your organizer and clip the coupon. To find out what items are on sale or even

FREE with a coupon, click on "CouponMom" at CouponCodeWorld.com.

Visit local stores regularly

Some of the best deals are never mentioned on CouponMom site or in the weekly sales ad. You should occasionally browse each aisle of your local supermarket. There could be real bargains located in discrete areas of the store. Ask the customer service desk where you can find the clearance spots and check those places. You'll score big savings when you match a coupon with clearance close out items.

Keep track of sales cycles

Stores repeatedly put the same items on sale. You will consistently save money if you know when to expect certain products to get marked down. Simply write down in notebook or spreadsheet program the dates when items you frequently purchase are on sale. Order extra coupons from coupon clipping services 1-2 weeks in advance of when you think a specific item's price will drop based on your tracking notes.

Make a shopping list ahead of time

People who go into supermarket without a shopping list are doomed from the start. Don't make this common mistake!

If you use a shopping list you'll avoid overspending and get out of the store much faster. It's critical that your shopping list specifies each item you plan to purchase, sale price, matching coupon discount, and anticipated check out total. Also, you should compile your shopping list based on the layout of store. Organize the items on your list by category (meat, dairy, bread/cereal, snacks/candy, paper goods, personal hygiene, cleaning supplies, health&beauty, miscellaneous items, etc).

To print a basic shopping list, visit CouponCodeWorld.com and click on "Print Grocery Shopping" list. You can fill in your own items and use it on future shopping trips.

Know the store policy for coupons

There is nothing more frustrating than to arrive at checkout with your coupons ready to score those sweet savings only to get this instead: "you've reached the maximum coupon limit" or "we don't accept internet coupons". Other people waiting behind you will give nasty looks. You may have to either put things back or pay full price. Not a pleasant experience!

The store coupon policy is often online. Visit the store website and click on "Coupon Policy" and print it. Bring the policy along when you shop. Some cashiers don't even know the store policy. The coupon policy for leading grocery store chains is included in the back section of *Extreme Savings* for easy reference.

Make sure the store has the items on your list

People visit the supermarket expecting every item on their shopping list to be in stock.

But in reality you might leave the store without several items on your list. Sometimes new items are hard to find at local stores. You actually do have more influence than you might think over the availability of store items.

The majority of supermarkets have a system in place that allows shoppers to request specific items or extra quantities for a big shopping trip. Ask the store manager to pre-order items you want to stockpile so you won't have to worry about those things being out of stock on the day you shop.

How to Stack Coupons for Extreme Savings

"Stacking" refers to the practice of combining coupons with the sale price of an item reducing the item's price even more. "Stacking" is the core of Extreme Couponing. You could possibly get several items for FREE or make a profit.

Here are a few examples:

Let's say CVS has a special where if you buy Nivea Bodywash for $3.99 you get a bonus $3.99 ExtraBuck. If you print a $4.00 off coupon for Nivea Bodywash at CouponCodeWorld.com and then grab another ten coupons for $4.00 off you have stashed away in your coupon organizer and use them all on the Nivea, you'll walk out of CVS with 11 FREE bottles of Nivea and $7.98 in ExtraBucks (assuming there is a limit of 2 ExtraBucks coupons).

So where do you get all of those coupons for Nivea?

Remember, if you are buying extra Sunday newspapers each week you will have those Nivea coupons in your coupon organizer!

You can stack in-store coupons with manufacturer coupons as well. Let's say that Target has General Mills cereal on sale for $1.99 and you have ten $1.00 off coupons for General Mills cereal. You're probably thinking "ok, the coupons will bring the cereal down to 99 cents...that's good". Well, another $1.00 off printable coupon at Target.com is going to make this good deal better:

General Mills Cereal
Sale Price: $1.99 - $1.00 manufacturer Coupon (x10)
- $1.00 Target Coupon (x10) = 10 FREE General Mills Cereals

You know when you get 10 boxes of cereal for FREE that's not just good, that's absolutely GREAT!

The in-store printable coupon made the General Mills Cereal FREE. You can duplicate this with several products if you visit a store's web site to print online coupons.

Remember, you can pair manufacturer coupons with online in-store coupons for Extreme Savings!

How to make regular priced items go on sale

You can actually get the price of an item lowered at stores such as Walmart and Target. Both retailers will match a competitor's advertised sales price on identical items.

Price Matching Example:

Hefty garbage bags (45ct) are advertised in the CVS/Pharmacy circular for $4.99, but Sally prefers to shop at Walmart where the Hefty bags are regularly priced $7.99. That's a $3.00 price difference. Walmart will actually match the CVS/Pharmacy sale price. If Sally shows the Walmart cashier the CVS/Pharmacy circular, she would get those Hefty bags for $4.99 and save $3.00.

Sally will save more when she stacks coupon with price match.

Here's how the final savings will look:

Hefty Garbage Bags
Reg Price: $7.99 - $3.00 (Price Match Savings)
- $2.00 (Manufacturer Coupon) = $2.99

Our shopper scored a sweet 67% discount with the price match and $2.00 off coupon.

Simple steps for successful price matching:

1. Browse through all the grocery store ads in Sunday newspaper.

2. Circle items you want to buy in each ad (Use highlighter). Write down those items on your shopping list as well. Also, match coupons in your coupon organizer with items on your shopping list.

3. Bring along the store ads when you shop at Target or Walmart. Don't cut out up the ads. You must leave ads in-tact because cashier will verify ad dates. You may only use current ads.

4. When you get to checkout, put the items you want price matched on front of belt.

5. Ask the cashier to price match any identical items that are priced lower elsewhere. Show cashier each item you highlighted in the competitor store ads. Remember to hand over your coupons.

6. The cashier will change prices to exact same low prices in the other store ads and deduct coupons.

7. SMILE. You just saved a bundle of money!

You don't have to drive all around town to different stores trying to score that one incredible deal. Instead use the price match strategy to save more time and much more money.

How to Master $5 off 10 items deals

You may have seen a supermarket advertise something to the likes of "save $5.00 when you buy 10 items". This kind of promotion is designed to reel you into store with hopes you will purchase much more than 10 items, preferable regular priced items outside the realm of the promotion. However, if you do the exact opposite of what the supermarket really wants you to do you will always come out saving money!

Let's say that the store will give you $5 off when you purchase 10 items in any combination from the following brand categories:

General Mills Cereal (Sale Price: $2.99)
Pepsi 2 Liters (Sale Price: $1.39)
Stouffer's Frozen Meals (Sale Price: $2.49)
Oscar Mayer Lunch Meat (Sale Price: $2.79)
Vitamin Water (Sale Price: $1.25)
Tide Detergent (32 loads) (Sale Price: $8.99)
Kraft Salad Dressing (Sale Price: $1.99)

The first thing you need to remember is that you're not limited to saving $5 off 10 items. You can buy 40 participating items and save $20.00. If you buy 80 items you will save $40.00 and so on. Focus on quantity. You want to get the most items for the least amount of money. You can do this by identifying the lowest priced and highest priced item. In this example the Vitamin water (Sale Price: $1.25) and Tide (Sale Price: $8.99) are focal points.

After simple math you can see that your dollar will be stretched further if you buy 10 Vitamin Water drinks at a total cost of $7.50. You can't even buy one bottle of the Tide for $7.50. You would scratch the Tide (highest priced item) from your shopping list. You can catch Tide on sale without the $5 off 10 items special.

So the Vitamin Water is on the list because it's the least expensive and Tide Detergent is out. The next thing you want to consider is your coupon inventory.

Let's say your coupon matches look like this here:

General Mills Cereal (10 - $1.00 Off Coupons)
Pepsi 2 Liters (No Coupons)
Stouffer's Frozen Meals (No Coupons)
Oscar Mayer Lunch Meat (10 - 75 Cents Off Coupons)
Vitamin Water (10 - $1.00 Off Coupons)
Kraft Salad Dressing (10 - $1.00 Off Coupons)

Pepsi and Stouffers are much less appealing because they have no matching coupons. Also, Pepsi is frequently on sale for 99 cents or less anyway. So there is no real incentive to keep Pepsi on the shopping list.

We are left with the following items:

General Mills Cereal
Oscar Mayer Lunch Meat
Vitamin Water
Kraft Salad Dressing

The next step is to decide what items on your narrowed down list you want to stockpile (buy in bulk).

Consider these questions when choosing items to stockpile:

How long will items last?

Don't bother stockpiling items that will quickly perish. The shelf life for cereal is usually several months. If cereal is among items on your short list stockpile it. Expect milk to last about 1 week pass the "sell by" date. Of course milk is perishable. But, it qualifies as a stockpile item because you could freeze it 1-2 months. However, avoid freezing milk after the "sell by" date. Put milk in freezer as soon as you get home from grocery store.

Will you use actually use the item?

People often load up on advertised items just to qualify for the $5.00 off 10 discount knowing they don't really need those items. There is no reason to buy items you will not enjoy regardless of the price. The Vitamin Water was selected as a best buy in this example. But, if you don't like the taste of Vitamin Water that item shouldn't be on your list with the only exception being you could give it to someone else that likes Vitamin Water. Now if you frequently eat salad at work or home the salad dressing would be a good item to stockpile. So focus on items that you will use.

Buy participating items with matching coupons

Sometimes the participating items in the $5 off 10 promotions are really not that great of a deal. The Pepsi 2 Liters are on sale for $1.39 and the price drops to 89 cents if you buy 10. That's not impressive if you can get the Pepsi next week for 99 cents regardless if your buy two or ten. Stick with items you have a coupon for that will bring down the price.

Let's take a look at how the final checkout will look with matching coupons for our $5 off 10 items special:

General Mills Cereal (Sale Price: $2.99)
Buy 10 | Sub Total=$29.90 - $5.00 (Promo)
- $10.00 (Manufacturer Coupons) = $14.90
Price Per Unit: $1.49 (Avg)

Oscar Mayer Lunch Meat (Sale Price: $2.79)
Buy 10 | Sub Total=$27.90 - $5.00 (Promo)
- $7.50 (Manufacturer Coupons) = $15.40
Price Per Unit: $1.54 (Avg)

Vitamin Water (Sale Price: $1.25)
Buy 10 | Sub Total=$11.25 - $5.00 (Promo)
- $10.00 (Manufacturer Coupons) = $3.75 (Credit)
Price Per Unit: $0.00 (Free)

Kraft Salad Dressing (Sale Price: $1.99)
Buy 10 | Sub Total=$19.90 - $5.00 (Promo)
- $10.00 (Manufacturer Coupons) = $4.90
Price Per Unit: $0.49 (Avg)

By stacking coupons with the $5 off 10 items promotion the average price of each item drastically dropped. You've got FREE drinks and condiments. Also, the above items will help slash your dining-out expenses. You could eat cereal and homemade lunches instead of restaurant meals.

Double Coupon Savings

Some stores will double the face value of coupons, which refers to "Double Coupons". Extreme Couponers shop at supermarkets that "Double Coupons". They frequently get stockpiles of FREE items thanks to "Double Coupons". Let's say that a local supermarket will double coupons valued up to 50 cents. They have SoftSoap, Reynolds Foil, Colgate Toothpaste each on sale for $1.00.

Great, you've got 30 coupons valued at 50 cents for each of those products in your coupon organizer, and every single coupon will be doubled at checkout.

Grab the coupons stashed away in your coupon organizer good for 50 cents off SoftSoap, Reynolds Foil, and Colgate; you will walk out of the supermarket with over 90 FREE items including enough toothpaste to last a very long time!

You can replicate this example as long as you focus on matching coupons that double with items already on sale. To find out what stores in your area will double coupons, click on "Grocery Store Ads" at CouponCodeWorld.com. Read the store's double coupon policy before you make up a shopping list.

Coupon Profits

Occasionally the value of your coupon will exceed item price, and when this occurs you actually make a profit on the coupon. The store might apply the difference to your check out bill. This is how extreme couponers leave stores with boatloads of free groceries.

For example, you have twenty coupons each for $5 dollar off a bottle of Maalox. You got these coupons from a coupon clipping service. Maalox is on sale for $3.00 at the local supermarket, so if you pick up 20 bottles of Maalox and use your twenty $5.00 off coupons on the Maalox, you'll have a credit balance of $40.00.

You can use the credit toward $40.00 worth of FREE meat, seafood, veggies, whatever you want! **So much for the old myth that says you can't get anything but junk food with coupons.**

About Coupon Print Limits

You should always attempt to print as many online coupons as possible. Hit the back arrow on your browser and try printing an additional coupon. If it works great, but don't stop at just two coupons. Yes, you will see a "Print Limit Reached" message after you attempt to print more than two coupons. But, this doesn't mean you can't get additional coupons. It's basically saying that you've reached the limit on that particular computer. No Problem! Use other computers in your house to print more coupons. If you have access to a computer at work or local library you can use those other computers to print more coupons.

However, you should never rely on fraudulent tactics such as copying coupons or creating counterfeit coupons to get extras. It's ethically wrong and illegal. Stay within the rules!

Ready To Go Shopping?

As you've learned there are ample sources for coupons. If you take full advantage of all the methods previously mentioned for building your coupon inventory, you'll have the tools necessary to save money. First use free sources to get coupon savings: Internet, coupon forums, manufacturer direct, loyalty programs, etc. After you wear out the free sources, consider paid sources such as clipping services, multiple newspaper subscriptions, entertainment book, etc. Extreme Savings is far from a walk in the park. It takes considerable amount of time and dedication to get those awesome deals. Some people spend 40 hours per week on coupons. That's like working a full time job.

Also, you could find yourself with the logistical challenge of where to keep things you accumulate.

Allocate enough space for your stockpile. Organize everything so expiring items rotate out. Write down the expiration date on items with a highlighter so they are clearly marked. Remember to use everything or donate items nearing expiration date to charity.

Congrats you now have the basic fundamentals of Extreme Savings. If you commit to using all the tips discussed in this section, you will consistently save allot of money and get freebies every time you shop.

But, you don't always have to go for that basket full groceries for $1.00 or keep a huge warehouse of items in an effort to achieve "Extreme Couponer" status. If you just save 20% off on your total checkout at the supermarket you're doing fine!

Now let's move on beyond grocery coupons.

How to Save Money Everyday

Eat for FREE!

Go online right now to: www.CouponCodeWorld.com and click on "Free Meals". Sign up for the eClubs of your favorite restaurants. You will find yourself eating for FREE maybe later today or tomorrow, and on your birthday and several days throughout the year. These places will give you freebies so they can establish and maintain a long-term relationship with you.

Some restaurants offer a loyalty card. You will usually get a FREE menu item (no purchase necessary) when you activate it online. Also, you earn points toward free meals when you present it. The leading restaurant loyalty card programs include Qdoba Mexican Grill, TGI Fridays, and Panera Bread. You'll find several more at CouponCodeWorld.com (Click on "eClub programs")

But, take measures to control your relationship with these places. Enter an alternate email address (for coupon emails) when you sign-up for the eClubs because you might get bombarded with email messages. If the company is sending you junk, opt-out of email communications by clicking "unsubscribe" link.

Let Kids Eat Free!

It might cost a small fortune when you bring kids along for dinner out. But, several restaurants offer Kids Eat Free promotions. You just need to know when and where these specials are going on.

You can get this info at KidsMealDeals.com. The site will help you pinpoint Kids Eat Free deals in your local area. The list includes small local diners and national restaurant chains.

Also, you don't have to order from that kids menu. You can order a generous adult entree and share a portion of it with the kids. You will also save about 10% - 15% off when you order water instead of soda. Skip the appetizers and you'll save more money.

Buy Generic Store Brands

You can save up to 65% off without a coupon when you purchase store brand. Buy the store brand when you are shopping for basic products like seasonings, foil, sugar, and garbage bags.

Many of the name brand companies actually make those cheaper store brands. The store brand is located on bottom shelf because brand name companies pay supermarkets money to place their products up higher. It has nothing to do with quality.

A bottle of store brand window cleaner will work fine. It has the same active ingredients as Windex. The only real difference between most store brand and name brand items is a bloated price for the name brand.

You'll save 30% or more when you buy store brands!

Who to shop with at supermarket?

The best person to go shopping with is YOU. If possible shop while your kids are in school. Kids will likely influence you to spend more money. The grocery stores realize that kids want everything that looks YUMMY. The grocery stores strategically place candy, pop, and other goodies where kids can easily grab those products. Those little goodies will disrupt your budget. Also, if you refuse to buy something your kid grabs, you know what will happen "huge meltdown" in front of other shoppers. Not Fun.

Try to choose a time when you can shop alone. But, if you must bring someone make it clear to the person that you will only buy what is on your shopping list.

Shop Clearance

The clearance area of a store is potential goldmine for money-saving deals. Always ask at the customer service desk where to find clearance items.

Grocery stores typically have designated spots in the store for clearance or marked down items including canned goods, dry goods, cookware, utensils, etc. Look for the items marked "Manager's Special" which typically includes milk, meat, cheese and juice. You can score incredible deals when you combine your coupons with these already low prices.

Always do the math

Several manufacturers have shrunk the contents of their products in an effort to boost profit margins. Two boxes of cereal may look similar in size but one box will frequently have less inside than the other. Can you determine which of the following is a better deal?

Kellogg's Cereal (18oz) on sale for $3.12
Versus
Kellogg's Cereal (25.5oz) on sale for $3.50

At first glance the $3.12 cereal looks cheaper than the $3.50 box based on the price tag. But, if you look pass the price tag and zoom in on that tiny price per unit cost number next to the price tag, you'll notice that the 25.5 oz box is cheaper at 14 cents per ounce versus 17 cents per ounce for the 18 oz box cereal. Also, you would get about 30% more cereal in that $3.50 box if you pay an extra 38 cents for the 25.5 oz box. By the way the price per unit is strategically tiny because the store will make more money when you shop products based on the retail price in larger print rather than price per ounce.

Kraft Easy Mac Cup (2.05oz) on sale 10/$10.00
Versus
Kraft Mac 'n cheese Box (6oz) on sale 2/$3.00

So lets do some simple math here. The price per unit on the Kraft Easy Mac Cup is 48 cents per ounce (wow, that's pricey) versus 25 cents per ounce on the Kraft Mac 'n cheese box. Although the $1.00 price tag on Kraft Easy Mac Cup is lower the price per ounce is nearly 50% higher than the Kraft Mac 'n cheese box. You pay more for the convenience of tossing the Easy Mac Cup in microwave for a fast snack. But, is this convenience worth it? You will get several bowls out of one box of Mac 'n cheese. Also, it's simple to make a box of Mac 'n cheese. You could store leftovers in your fridge ready to grab for a quick snack.

You can easily do the math on products!

Use that little calculator function on your cellphone to figure out cost per unit. Divide item price by number of ounces or pieces in the pack. For example, if one brand of diapers is $17.49 and there are 66 in the box and a different brand is $15.99 and it has 60 in the box you would punch this into your calculator:

Brand 1: $17.49 ÷ 66 = .26 cents per diaper

Brand 2: $16.99 ÷ 60 = .28 cents per diaper

As you can see diaper Brand 1 actually cost less than Brand 2 despite the higher price tag of $17.49.

Remember, to pay close attention to the price per unit!

How to score the best shopping deals

Stores will often mark down items because they have a holiday design. Sometimes a fine box of chocolates regular priced $18.00 will have Santa on the package forcing the store to mark it down to $3.00 or less. But, it's the same delectable chocolate in that package priced at $18.00. Retailers stock their shelves with themed seasonal items only to slash the price to near nothing on those items later. You'll find plenty of awesome deals if you shop the day after Halloween, Easter, 4th of July, and of course the granddaddy of them all Christmas.

When to shop for the best deals

If you know when prices on items are going to be slashed you will NEVER pay full price for anything!

These are prime times for great savings:

January

Holiday Decor: Christmas is over. Retailers practically giveaway merchandise around this time. You can stock up on wrapping paper, lighting ornaments, etc for the holiday season next year.

Exercise Equipment: Fitness stores will roll out nice discounts to bring in the countless numbers of people who make a New Years weight loss resolution.

LCD HDTVs: Be on the look out for rock bottom deals enticing you to watch the BIG GAME on a BIG screen. TVs will go on-sale again around NCAA March Madness and day after Thanksgiving.

February

Perfume Fragrances: Raid Walgreens and CVS the day after Valentines Day. They always markdown their boxed fragrance sets. Ask the cosmetics clerk to point you toward the deals.

March

Winter Clothing: You'll find leather jackets, thermal coats, gloves, and more marked down up to 95% off. This stuff must go to make room for Spring lineup. Stockpile for next winter!

Frozen Food Deals: March is National Frozen Food Month. Watch your mail for money saving coupons from leading frozen food brands including Tyson, Green Giant, On-Cor, Jimmy Dean and more. Visit www.easyhomemeals.com for details.

April

Digital Cameras: They will be marked down for people ready to take off for spring break.

Summer Clothing: It's not quite Summer in April, but department stores will have warm weather clothing with teaser markdowns.

May

Cookware Sets: Retailers will unleash aggressive discounts to grab consumers shopping for wedding gifts and Mother's Day.

Barbecue: May is National Barbecue Month. There will be plenty of promotions. You can score great deals at local area barbeque places, and discounts on anything related to barbeque in general.

June

Ice Cream: June is when the dairy industry celebrates everything dairy. You can get the scoop on where to find free sundaes and other cool savings at www.nationaldairycouncil.org

Tools & Electronics: Look for savings on gadgets for grads and tool gift sets for dads.

July

Home Furniture: The American Home Furnishings Alliance says July is when furniture stores roll out big discounts to unload excess inventory. So if you are thinking about buying a new couch July is the right time to shop for one.

Bye Bye Summer. Department stores must push out Summer items to make room for back to school and winter items. You'll see some sweet deals on shorts, t-shirts, beech wear, and apparel.

August

School supplies, fall clothing, laptops: August rules when it comes to back-to-school deals. You will benefit from competitive pricing among retailers. Walmart and Office Depot usually have the best deal on laptops. You can save big on ink pens, markers, and crayons at Walgreens and CVS/Pharmacy.

Lawn & Outdoor Products: When the temperature falls so will prices. Look for deals on lawnmowers, gardening products, air conditioners, and summer outdoor items. Pack it all up, and you won't have to pay full price for those items next Summer.

September

Look for sweet Labor Day deals on bedding, appliances, and last minute back to school bargains.

Cars: The new models will hit showrooms. Dealers want to get rid of those older models. So you will be in a really good bargaining position. Last year's model is considered "older" by dealerships.

October

Pizza: October is National Pizza Month. Look for deals on Pizza. Did you know 94% of Americans eat Pizza at lease once a month?

Home Appliances: The new washer and dryers models will arrive in stores. Last year's models will be marked down to make room.

Grills: Walmart will bump their grilling section for Christmas merchandise so prices will plunge.

November

Wedding and Prom Dresses: It's dead in boutiques. So they will offer great markdowns to get rid of inventory. Stick the dress in your closet until the big day arrives.

Clothing, Video Game Consoles, Tablets: You already know Black Friday is the day after Thanksgiving and retailers need to turn their profit margins from red to black. You will find door-busters and incredible deals to kick off the holiday shopping season. Be sure to view leaked Black Friday ads at www.theblackfriday.com or www.thanksgivingblackfridayads.com

Also, several stores will give you a price adjustment if the item goes on sale within seven days. So visit one of the leaked ad websites and find out what items will be on sale. If you notice that a specific item you want will be included in the Black Friday sale buy it at regular price. Bring back the item along with your receipt to get an adjustment. This beats waiting in a mile long line at the crack of dawn to get those door buster deals.

Don't forget "Cyber Monday" which is when online retailers offer incredible deals, "Cyber Monday" is Monday after Thanksgiving.

December

Year-End Car Bargains: Dealers are under pressure to get cars off the lot to avoid certain inventory expenses. So haggle for a price 2% - 10% below sticker. You can use ConsumerReports.com car buying service to find out dealer holdback amount. This information will give you leverage when negotiating car price.

Toys and Games: Plethora of deals to put you in the shopping spirit. You've held out until this moment. It's time to go for it!

How to stretch your grocery food dollars

Freeze It!

If you don't have an extra box freezer in your house, please get one asap. It's worth the investment. You can stockpile when supermarket is running a great sale on essentials (meat, bread, milk, etc). Store it all in your freezer!

Don't hold back on items with a close "sell-by" date on package.

Grocery stores frequently mark down items that are near sell-by date. But, you can store things in your freezer 1-2 months pass the specified sell-by date. So if you see a good sale on milk, stockpile!

Portion foods: meat, fruits, and cheese.

You can stretch your dollar by cutting meat into sections for each meal. Lets say that you buy 4 pounds of ground beef for $8.00. If you cut the meat into 4 sections you will have broken down the price to about $2.00 per meal. Store meat in your freezer for later use. When you are ready to prepare a meal grab some ground beef out of your freezer.

Also, just because a recipe calls for 1 pound of meat doesn't mean you have to put a pound in there. You can use a third or half

pound. It will taste great and you'll save money by using less meat. You can supplement the meal with veggies.

How to save on cheese

You pay a premium whenever you buy pre-packed sliced or shredded cheese. You can save 10% - 30% off when you buy cheese by the block. Those kinds of savings are well worth the few minutes it will take to grate your own cheese.

Use recyclable shopping bags

Several retailers will reward you for using green bags. For example CVS/Pharmacy will give you a $1.00 off coupon every 4th time you buy something and put the items in a recyclable bag. You just buy the bag and reuse it. Target will give you a 5-cent discount if you pack groceries in your own bags. Aldi stores charge for their bags so you can save money by bringing your own bags. This will help the environment and help you save money!

Warehouse Savings

We previously revealed that the real cost of an item is "price per ounce". If you believe in the idea of shopping based on "quantity" head over to your nearest warehouse store. They sell the same items available in supermarkets, but in bulk at a much lower price. Sam's Club and Costco are well known places to stock up on paper towels, cereal, dry foods, cheese, etc. Just about anything you can imagine. You do have to pay an annual membership fee. If you want to avoid a membership fee, try GFS Marketplace outlets (visit "GFS.com online to find the nearest location).

GFS Marketplace does not require a membership fee. They carry a variety of bulk food items similar in value to items at Sam's Club and Costco.

Dollar Store Savings

The Dollar Tree chain of stores is a great place to find everyday items such as cleaning supplies, school supplies, toothpaste, etc for just $1.00. Dollar Tree carries name brand items priced twice as much in grocery stores. You will really come out like a bandit around holidays. Dollar Tree has wrapping paper, greeting cards, and materials to make nice gift baskets.

To locate nearest Dollar Tree store visit: www.dollartree.com

Freecycle Network

The Freecycle Network is a non-profit group of people that give each other free stuff in an effort to prevent items from getting into land fields. Freecycle Network offers a wide assortment of useful items. You can post "wanted" items on the website. To find the nearest Freecycle group, visit www.freecycle.org

How to get cashback on everything

Use a credit card that pays you to shop!

Many credit cards offer as high as 5% cashback on purchases at supermarkets, drug stores, gas stations, auto repair, and more. A 5% cashback deal is equivalent to a 5% discount on your purchases. If you use a cashback credit card for your routine purchases, that can turn into significant savings over the course of the year. Here are few cashback cards to consider:

Paypal Debit Mastercard

With the Paypal Debit Mastercard you will earn 1% cashback on your purchases (Groceries, Gas, Online Shopping..). 1% cashback may not sound like much on the surface but those little 1% cashback bonuses will accumulate very fast if you consistently use the card on all of your purchases. The Paypal Debit Mastercard is 100% FREE with no crazy fees. All you need is a Paypal account. You can sign up for a free Paypal account at www.Paypal.com

Target RedCard

Target offers a debit and credit card that will give you 5% cashback on purchases. You are allowed to stack coupons on top of that 5% cashback discount. Target also send their cardholders special bonus coupons in the mail. So head over to Target.com or your nearest Target store and sign-up for a Target RedCard.

You should attempt to get a card with no annual fees. But, even if the card does have an annual of fee of $35.00 or whatever you will still be fine. As long as you get free airline miles or cashback money that exceeds the annual fee it's worth it.

Pay off your balance each month. Don't ever allow the monthly credit balance to exceed 10% of your monthly income. You'll come out ahead as long as you keep your balance near zero to avoid financing charges. The credit card company will not close your account if you never carry a balance. They are already making money off people who do carry a balance and pay interest fees.

To compare cashback cards, visit bankrate.com. cardratings.com, or cardhub.com

Comparison shop before you buy anything!

Thanks to fierce competition in today's retail industry you can truly get the best price on virtually anything you want to purchase. You need to imprint a "price comparison calculator" in you mind that is running at all times. You should always be thinking "how much would this cost elsewhere". If it's over 5% cheaper elsewhere go elsewhere to buy it. Grocery stores now offer their circulars online, so check the Internet ads prior to shopping. Remember, Walmart and Target will price match if you show competitor ad.

Before you break out your wallet to buy that incredibly marked down item, visit a price comparison website. Search how much it's selling for online at various retailers. Check prices at pricegrabber.com or netpersonalshopper.com. You may find that an item is priced much cheaper with free shipping and no sales tax. You can compare prices right on the spot with Google Shopper App. The Google Shopper App allows you to scan barcode of any item with your phone. It will instantly display how much the item is selling for at local and online stores.

Google Shopper App offers product user reviews, specifications, and other key information. Search for "Google Shopper App" in Smartphone apps store.

The pendulum does swing both ways. Online retailers may claim to have the lowest price on a particular item you want to purchase. But that item might actually be cheaper at big box store. It doesn't hurt to call local stores and check prices.

How to get a bargain on practically anything

The price tag is not necessarily the amount you have to pay for an item. There is often room for price negotiation on items and services such as furniture, appliances, auto repair, etc.

Steps to successful price negotiation (aka "haggling"):

1. **Don't say something like "is it okay if you…lower the price a bit?".** They won't think it's okay to lower the price. They want the highest possible price. You will likely get an emphatic "NO" to that open-ended question. Instead say point blank what you want to pay. For example, if the price of an item is $550.00 but you prefer to pay $495.00 then politely say "I could pay $495.00 for it").

The $495.00 offer in this scenario equates to a 10% discount, which is within the range of leeway most sales reps are allowed to accept. But if the sales rep is reluctant to cooperate then ask to speak with a manager. The manager has more flexibility to reduce the price. So get in the habit of offering 10% - 20% below whatever price you see on tag.

2. **Don't show the love**. You immediately lose upper hand if you express utter desire for something. Instead convey only lukewarm interest. Project an attitude that will alert the seller that you are willing to leave without the item if they refuse to drop price.

3. **Bring cash**. Credit card companies charge merchants a transaction fee when customers use credit card. They don't like to pay those swipe fees. The manager or sales rep might be more willing to accept your offer if you stress that you will pay cash. In fact, open your wallet and start counting out money. They won't want that money going back into your wallet.

4. **Do your homework**. Check online price comparison sites, such as Google Shopping and PriceGrabber.com, and look at newspaper sales ads. Show the salesperson any lower online prices for the item elsewhere. The sales rep will probably either match the price or throw in some extra freebies.

The above tips will immediately help you save real money. Here are ideal places to negotiate for lower prices.

Local Mom and Pop Stores

Yardsales

Pawnshops

Car Dealerships

Mattress Stores

Flea Markets

Mall Kiosk Shops

Auto Repair Shops

Service Provider Savings

Always hunt for the best price with service providers. Get at least two quotes with any service work required on your car, house, etc. Explain what you need done over the phone. **Ask upfront what they charge per hour for labor.** The cost of labor is what matters the most. Choose the lowest quote.

This goes for legal services too. If you ever must hire a lawyer, you should speak with two or three lawyers and negotiate their compensation. Do this regardless if the person is a friend or family member. Compare rates whenever you need to hire a service provider. You'll find the price gaps astonishing.

Read reviews!

If you pay close attention to reviews you will avoid wasting money on something with known issues. Dozens of review websites allow consumers to post "pros" and "cons" of a product. It's a safe bet to purchase a product with a 4 or 5 star review rating. But, if the reviews are overwhelmingly bad stay clear of that product. For example, front load washers are heralded as water bill savers but some models vibrate loud and furiously.

A good source for consumer reviews is Consumer Reports. The magazine provides unbiased reviews on home appliances, electronics, baby products, computers, and more. Also, you don't necessarily have to buy the magazine or join one of those review sites that ask you to pay membership fee. You can read reviews absolutely FREE. Just google "reviews" for the product you want to purchase. Read reviews for service providers as well.

How to get free stuff for your child's school

You can help your child's school receive free supplies and equipment when you turn in specially marked labels located on products you buy frequently.

You may notice Box Tops For Education" symbol on a box of cereal or heard something about the program. If you turn in those little "Box Tops For Education" labels the school will earn points redeemable for FREE equipment, computers, and so much more!

However, "Box Tops For Education" is not the only program designed to help schools. Others include Campbell's Labels for Education, My Coke Rewards for Schools, and Tyson Project A+. Find a place to store those labels and give them to the local pta.

To learn more about the various education label programs, visit CouponCodeWorld.com and click on "You can make a difference!"

How to save money on work lunch breaks

The best ways to save money is to take your lunch to work. Cutting those expensive lunch meals from your budget will save you as much as $200.00 each month. There are many other lunch options. You can choose from an assortment of tasty sandwiches.

You might have chicken salad sandwich one day and peanut butter sandwich the next. Mixing up your sandwich choices will help keep you from feeling like you're daily lunch routine is boring.

How to save on cable, movies, and music

Satellite TV Savings

Last year millions of Americans dropped digital cable for satellite tv. Digital Cable cost on average about $65.00 per month. The price of two leading satellite tv providers Dish Network and DirectTV is about 20% - 30% less than Digital Cable. You'll save more when you order the least expensive basic package.

The other higher priced programming packages are bloated with channels you may not desire. So if you don't need the extra channels then don't shell out more money for a premium package. Also, the satellite tv providers usually offer a $100 gift card or other incentive to steal customers away from cable. You should get a free gift card or something when you sign-up with a local satellite agent. But if they don't offer you a bonus, look for better deal. There are several satellite tv agents to choose from. Find one that will offer you FREE installation with NO activation fees.

Satellite tv is much cheaper than cable, but some people prefer digital cable to satellite and will never switch over, which is understandable. You can still save money without canceling cable tv. You could save 5% - 10% on your bill if you pick up the phone and ask the cable company for a lower rate that will better fit your budget. This doesn't mean you have to change your programming package. They might give you a discount for switching from paper to online billing. The cable company likely will offer you discount because they want to keep you subscribed. Call them today and ask for a better deal.

To compare prices on cable and satellite in your area, visit www.WhiteFence.com or BillShrink.com.

Cut your Movie Expenses with Netflix

Netflix is the leading Internet subscription service for streaming movies and tv shows. With Netflix you can have movies zapped right to your tv for dirt cheap.

In fact, people are dropping paid tv all together in favor of Netflix. Netflix's most popular plan cost about $8.99 per month. That's an incredible value in comparison to the average cable and satellite bill. Netflix includes a huge collection of over 100,000 titles allowing serious movie buffs to access a wide range of classic movie title categories. Also, you have more control over your viewing choices. A Netflix night coupled with ACT II Microwave Popcorn is a great alternative to that night out at the movie theater costing upwards to $35.00.

Try Netflix free for 2 weeks at Netflix.com.

Be sure to consider other movie rental services offered by Amazon.com, Vudu, Hula, CinemaNow, and Redbox.com. You can get one free movie rental each month when you sign-up for a Redbox account at Redbox.com

How to save Money on Movie Tickets

Yes, it's expensive to take your family to the movies. Netflix is indeed a cheaper alternative. But, you don't have to completely give up that fun time out at the movies. Several theaters offer special discount days allowing you to save on admission tickets and concessions. Regal Theaters, a leading movie chain offers $5.00 admission on certain days for all movies.

Also, you can get popcorn for just 2 bucks and earn FREE movie tickets, drinks, and popcorn when you join Regal Crown Club loyalty program. Other theater chains offer similar programs.

You will save money if you see movies during the week (Monday thru Thursday) rather than on the weekend. Think about it! Would it be a huge sacrifice to see a movie on Tuesday instead of Friday or Saturday? For more information about discount movie days, click on "Movie Theater Discounts" at CouponCodeWorld.com or visit the following sites:

www.REGmovies.com (Click on "Crown Club")
Regal Entertainment Group: Regal Cinemas, United Artist Theaters, Edwards Theaters

www.amcstubs.com
AMC Movie Theaters

www.ravemotionpictures.com/coupons.aspx
Rave Movie Theaters

www.marcustheatres.com/Promotion/
Marcus Theaters

www.cinemark.com/values-discounts.aspx
Cinemark Theaters

www.gohollywood.com
Hollywood Theaters (Hollywood Insider)

www.nationalamusements.com/programs/
National Amusements

www.harkinstheatres.com/onlyAtHarkins.aspx
Harkins Theaters

How to save on music

Buy music downloads!

You can instantly download entire records or just your favorite songs. The sound quality of mp3 songs are great and with hot titles priced under $1.00 it's a budget friendly alternative for music lovers. To find cheap mp3 songs online visit: Amazon.com, Walmart.com, or iTunes.com.

How to save Money at Home

Wouldn't it be great if they offered coupons in the Sunday newspaper for 50% off your home mortgage or rent payment or a coupon for FREE phone service?

Newspapers would sell like hot cakes. We all know that's not going to happen. But, you can indeed save quite a bit of money on your mortgage or rent payments, insurance, and other non-discretionary expenses.

Let's take a look at some ways to lower bills.

How to save on mortgage payments

Take advantage of low rates!

If your current mortgage payment is sucking up over 25% of your annual income you have to do something to reduce those payments. Don't allow high mortgage payments to keep you in financial bondage. Refinancing could be a good course of action to take provided your existing mortgage rate is above current interest rates. For example, you can save up to $500.00 per month by slashing your interest rate by 1% on a 30 year fixed mortgage. These savings might allow you to pay off your mortgage early. The sooner you get rid of that mortgage payment the sooner you will become debt free, which is a good thing!

But make sure that the monthly savings will exceed the total amount of fees associated with refinancing your mortgage. Potential Yearly Savings: $6,000.00.

Consider buying a HUD home

What is HUD Home?

Basically, a property becomes HUD home when the homeowner defaults on FHA-backed mortgage. In other words, when FHA-backed mortgages go through the foreclosure process, they become the property of HUD (US Department of Housing and Urban Development. This book is about saving money. The cost of purchasing a home is the biggest expense most families will ever encounter. You could save several thousands of dollars (up to 50% or more off market price) when you buy a HUD home. That's why HUD homes are mentioned in Extreme Savings.

You will have much **lower mortgage payment or no mortgage payment** if you purchase a HUD home. Many HUD homes have a stigma of being run down houses located in the poorest area of town, but that's not the case for every HUD home. In fact, you may be able to find a bargain HUD home in your preferred area. Of course you must think about the amount of money it will take to rehab HUD property.

A HUD home might serve as possible investment opportunity as well. You could flip (buy and resale) HUD home or rent it out for steady flow of extra rental income. This section won't discuss real estate investing in depth. But, if you are interested in learning more about real estate investing see "Additional Recourses" section located in the back of book.

There are services that charge a fee to search HUD properties. Don't fall for it! View properties FREE at Hud.gov

Negotiate for lower rent

The monthly rent for an apartment or house is not etched in stone. Simply ask your landlord for a reduction in rent when your lease is up for renewal. The landlord will likely work with you, because they don't want to get stuck with an empty unit no longer generating income. But, if the landlord refuses to lower your payments move to a cheaper place. You can find great deals such as "1-month free rent" by searching online. Rent.com offers a free $100 visa gift card when you use their website.

Also, remember that your rent payments should never exceed 30% of your total monthly income.

How to save on Insurance

Combine Insurance Policies.

You can save money on your insurance premium by consolidating coverage for car, life, home, and renter's with one provider. Also, you will save money if you pay your premium annually or semi-annually rather than month-to-month. Try to increase your insurance deductible. For example, if you raised your deductible from $500 to $1,000 you could save 25% or more on your insurance payments. You should keep at least $1,000 in an emergency fund to cover the deductible.

Occasionally shop for a better insurance rate even if you have been with your current provider for a while. If you find a lower rate, ask your insurance agent to match it. If they decline, switch to new insurance company.

To compare insurance rates, visit: www.netquote.com, www.insurance.com, or www.esurance.com

Also, doing little things such as not texting on your cell phone while at the wheel and defensive driving reduce the odds of being in accident, which is leading cause of sky-high insurance premiums. Potential Yearly Savings: $150.00 - $575.00

How to save on utilities

You could significantly reduce monthly heating and electricity bills by turning your home green. For starters, replace every incandescent bulb in your home with a compact fluorescent light bulb. The cfl bulbs use less electricity. It last about 10 times longer than incandescent bulbs. Also, install a programmable thermostat to maximize energy savings. It will help maintain comfortable temperature at peak times. You can save 5% - 20% off heating bill with programmable thermostat. That's money in the bank!

Don't allow heat to seep out of your house. Add extra insulation to drafty areas (walls, attic, doorways, etc) and replace old crackly windows with new energy efficient windows. This will keep heat in your house and money in your pocket.

Also, you may qualify to receive financial help paying your utility bills. You don't have to be dirt poor or on food stamps to get assistance. Contact your local township office or LIHEAP at 1 (866) 674-6327 to learn about bill payment assistance programs.

How to slash your water bill

You can reduce water bill by installing an aerator on your water faucets and showerheads. It screws on the bottom of the faucet reducing water flow without reducing water pressure. You can pick up aerators (Reg Price: $1.99 - $5.99) at a local hardware store.

Also, keep a pitcher of water in the fridge. This way you don't have to run water until it get cold.

Cut down the wait time for hot water.

You are wasting a ton of water if you routinely run your water for a while before it finally gets hot. Look into a "point-of-use hot water heater". It's an electric portable water heater. You hook it up under the faucet sink and water is heated instantly. They cost between $160.00 - $250.00 on Amazon.com. Worth the investment!

A dishwasher gulps water. Avoid pre-washing your dishes. Instead scrape food off plates and wash the dishes on primary cycle. If possible buy a front-loading cloths washer, which requires less water and spins cloths faster to reduce drying time.

These household improvements will cost money, but everything will eventually pay for itself overtime. You may qualify for tax credit worth up to $1,500 when you purchase "Energy Star" rated products including insulation, windows, new hot water heater, etc. To learn more about the "Energy Star" tax credit, visit: www.energystar.gov

How to save on your phone bill

Say Goodbye Landline Bill!

Nearly 17% of Americans only use cell phones. As the U.S. economy tightens, consumers are looking for ways to cut household spending. People are now eyeballing that landline phone bill, which averages $40.00 per month. Eliminate landline phone charges by using your cell phone as your primary phone.

Did you know that Google will give you a free phone number with free local phone service?

That's Right, you can get a free phone number and make free local phone calls through your computer by using GoogleTalk. The call sound quality is very good. To sign up for a free GoogleTalk account, visit: www.google.com/talk/

Another alternative is to use a free video calling service such as Skype or ooVoo.com.

Also, you might be able to get high-speed DSL with no phone service, which would cut 10% - 30% off your phone bill. This is a great way to save money if you really don't need phone line but want Internet service. Contact your local phone company to find out if they offer DSL without phone service.

Potential Yearly Savings: $1000.00
(vs. Landline Phone Service & Long-Distance Plans)

Cellphone Savings

If you don't have an unlimited texting plan, the cost of texting could cause your cellphone bill to surge. You can avoid text message charges by using free texting apps. Search on your phone for these free apps: TxtDrop, Textfree, or TextPlus.

Also, contact your cellphone provider. Find out the average number of minutes you've used over the past three months. Tell the cellphone company that you want to downgrade to a cheaper plan with minutes closer to your average usage.

Also, consider ordering your next cellphone online from another source besides your provider. You'll find much lower prices on popular cellphones at www.amazon.com.

How to get FREE PC and Video Games

There are thousands of fun and FREE games for kids and adults. Search "FREE GAMES" on your Android SmartPhone or iPhone. Also, you can play games on your computer for FREE at www.games.yahoo.com/free-games

GameFly video game rental service offers a FREE trial whereas you can try out hot video games (Xbox 360, PS3, Wii) absolutely FREE for 10-days. To get the coupon code, click on GameFly at CouponCodeWorld.com.

To see a list of popular FREE apps and games, click on FREE games at CouponCodeWorld.com. Potential Yearly Savings: $550.00 - $750.00+

Where to find money in your house

The easiest way to get some money out of things lying around the house is to have an online rummage sale. You can turn those rarely worn clothes, shoes, and gadgets you don't use into cash. Purge through everything in your house. Sell whatever you don't need on eBay or Craigslist. You can use the money to pay off debts and clear clutter at the same time. Potential Yearly Savings: $50.00 - $2,500.00+

How to save BIG on travel

Book air and hotel in advance

Avoid trying to get a flight or hotel room at the last minute. Yes, sometimes last minute deals are out there. But you might actually pay a higher price if you wait to book. Instead reserve everything 1 - 3 months in advance to get the best rate and ensure room availability. Hotwire.com is a great online service for rock bottom deals on airline tickets, hotels, and car rental. There is frequently a coupon for Hotwire.com in Entertainment Book.

Book over the phone

Travelers can land lower rates by booking over the phone at specific hotel branch as well. Ask to speak directly to hotel manager who might offer you special rates not advertised online. Also after booking a room, periodically call hotel to see if the rate for rooms have gone down since the reservation. If rates have dropped, you can cancel your reservation and rebook at the lower rate. Take into consideration peak travel times, holidays, and special events, which typically jack up rates.

Plan meals ahead of time

Most people decide where to eat on impulse "we'll just see what looks good" but that is a sure fire way to overspend. You will save money when you plot out your dining choices in advance.

If you are going on a road trip, decide where you will eat before you step into the car. Bring along your coupon organizer, which should be well stocked with restaurant coupons. Also, order an Entertainment Book for the city you are visiting. The Entertainment Book will have plenty of local discounts on food.

How to get FREE wireless internet

Many hotels will make you pay an extra $7 - $25 per night to have wireless Internet in your room. It's just another stream of fee based profits for the hotel. But, you can keep that money in your pocket by using FREE public wireless hot spots. There are usually dozens of them near hotels in every major city. Some of the common locations include Barnes & Noble, Panera Bread, college campuses, and public libraries. You can download a free hot spot locator app at www.JiWire.com

Enjoy FREE Attractions and Activities

There are numerous free activities to do in nearly all cities. You can visit the best museums and attractions on earth without a paying a dime. Leading free spots include the Smithsonian museums in Washington, D.C., the Getty Center in Los Angeles, CA and Lincoln Park Zoo and Millennium Park of Chicago, IL. Others such as the Indianapolis Children's Museum (arguably world's best) and Museum of Modern Art of New York will let you visit free of charge on certain days. Also, several colleges host free outdoor concerts, exhibits, and movie showings open to the general public. Many local restaurants and small shops frequently offer free samples and welcome gifts to tourist.

You just have to plan ahead and find out when and where to get these FREE deals and it's easy, Click on "FREE Things To Do" at CouponCodeWorld.com

Visit the Convention and Visitors Bureau website for the city you plan to visit. They offer free coupons and discounts for popular tourist points in town.

How to save on Parking

It's no big secret that parking is expensive and a pain in the "you know what". The best thing to do is compare rates and parking spots online before you venture into the city. You can do just that at bestparking.com and primoparking.com

Also, attempt to offer the parking attendant a lesser amount in cash. If the parking rate states $35.00, flash the attendant $25.00 in cash. They might accept your offer during off peak hours.

How to get a FREE vacation

If you are up for a little out door adventure, you should look into the USDA Forest Service - Passport in Time Program. It provides free tours of historical US forest sites and free lodging with full-service kitchen, showers and flush toilets, and meals for very little or no cost. **For more details visit: www.passportintime.com**

How to save on a car

Keep the car you have now.

If you own a high mileage car that still gets you from point a to b, don't rush into buying new car. You may have to spend money on normal maintenance, but you will enjoy life without that annoying car note to pay each month.

When you are ready for new wheels, shop online. You'll avoid the sales pressure filled atmosphere of a dealer showroom by shopping on your computer for a vehicle.

Yahoo Autos offers a free service you can use to search for cars It provides up to 3 quotes from area dealers. Simply choose the lowest price quote on the exact car you want to buy. To compare auto prices, visit: www.CouponCodeWorld.com and click on Buy "New / Used Car" at top of page.

Other Recommended Sites: www.cars.overstock.com, www.cars.com, www.autotrader.com, www.edmunds.com

Potential Yearly Savings: $1,100.00 - $6,500.00+

How to save on gas

You will save 2% - 10% on gas if you check prices online before you fill up at the pump. A good service to use is GasBuddy gas price comparison app. It will show you lowest gas price based on your zip code. Here's how to score the best gas price:

1. Visit CouponCodeWorld.com and click on "GasBuddy" or use Smartphone to access the app.

2. Click "Find Gas Near Me" button. GasBuddy will display lowest gas prices. It shows gas station addresses, distance, and last reported prices. Just fill up at whichever gas station that has the best price in your local area.

Other things to remember about GasBuddy

You'll earn a chance to win FREE gas when you report prices at GasBuddy.com

The reported Gasbuddy prices may change at any moment. It's very annoying to arrive at gas station only to find out the prices are not the same as reported on Gasbuddy. You will have better luck going to gas stations where the last reported Gasbuddy price is less than 1 hours old.

Don't attempt to check gas prices while you are driving. That's distractive and could cause a car accident. Instead use Gasbuddy before you get in car.

Use Gas Station Loyalty Card

Also, many leading gas station chains offer a free loyalty rewards card that will allow you to earn points when you purchase gas. Points are redeemable for FREE gas. The next time you visit your favorite gas station ask for loyalty card.

There are several credit cards on the market with little or no monthly fees that will give you 5% cashback on your gas purchases. The 5% cashback translates into a 5% discount on gas. You can compare gas credit cards at creditcards.com.

How to save on Health Care Cost

Use a flexible spending account (FSA)

If you don't already have a flexible spending account, speak with your employer about it. An FSA allows you to pay medical expenses (prescriptions, office co-pays, dental expenses, etc) with a special debit card. This money is deducted from your payroll check. The best part is that money withdrawn from your FSA is not subject to payroll taxes, so you'll have a lower tax bill. Be sure to monitor your FSA. Use all of the funds because you will lose any leftover money at end of the year. Potential Yearly Savings: $200.00 - $1,500.00+

Eat healthy and exercise!

Many health issues are related to weight. You will save on health care expenses if you maintain well balanced diet coupled with exercise. You don't have to join posh fitness club to reach healthy weight. Simply take walks every week, which is free to do!

Also, prepare meals at home to save money and gain control over what is going into your body. Fast food restaurants provide a cheap and convenient way to put meal on the table. But, you can really make healthier meals at home that taste ten times better than anything available at the drive-thru.

Crunched for time?

Easy Solution: Prepare meals on the weekend. Put it all in fridge. Just pop something in the microwave oven when it's time to feed your family. For quick mouthwatering recipes, visit www.cooks.com.

Be sure to read the nutritional value section on back of products. Avoid brands packed with calories, carbs, saturated fat, and sodium. All of that junk can lead to high cholesterol, which in turn is the recipe for heart disease. If you develop heart disease you will be heading toward possible coronary artery bypass surgery. The average cost of a bypass surgery is about $100,000. So it's well worth the effort to have a balanced health conscious diet. You will decrease your odds of ever developing heart disease. If all Americans commit to a healthy lifestyle, the cost of health care and insurance premiums will shrink across the board for everyone.

What you should know about Hospital Bills

A number of hospitals are indeed for profit. They want to admit patients and make as much money as possible. In fact, one of the largest hospital chains Health Management Associates, which operates 70 hospitals was investigated by 60 Minutes. During interviews with 60 Minutes, employees stated that HMA would "relentlessly" pressure doctors to admit people regardless of their medical need so the hospital could make more money. The doctor's were basically told if they didn't fill hospital beds they would lose their job. To learn more about this scandal, google "hospitals the cost of admission 60 minutes".

Many hospitals routinely charge outrageous fees for unnecessary tests and treatments, pills, etc. They might charge $70.00 for roll of gauze you could buy for a few bucks at Walmart.

Hospital pills are absurdly over priced. Author, Steven Brill wrote a telling article for Time Magazine titled "Bitter Pill: Why Medical Bills Are Killing Us" Search for the article online. It reveals the infamous "chargemaster" sheet. The "chargemaster" sheet is a detailed list of items billable to hospital patient. You won't believe markups.

If you must be admitted into hospital, go over your bill with a fine toothcomb. According to Medical Billing Advocates of America, a national association that reviews medical bills for consumers reports that 80 percent of hospital bills likely contain errors that may include:

Charging for an unnecessary service your doctor did not order.

Charging you for high priced brand name drugs when your doctor specified using a generic drug.

Charging you twice for a test if it was administered incorrectly the first time or if original test results were misplaced (not your fault, you shouldn't pay for their mistake).

Charging for excessive amount resulting from clerical errors due to entering the wrong code for a service or procedure.

If you feel that a mistake has occurred on your bill, contact the hospital billing department. If you can't handle the matter over phone, send them a letter detailing the mistake. Let your insurance company know about the suspected error as well.

For assistance with resolving medical bill issues, visit www. www.billadvocates.com

The problem of inflated charges in hospitals has not been properly addressed. If you want to voice your concerns, contact your local congress person at (202) 224-3121 or visit www.house.gov/representatives

Use urgent care center

The vast majority of emergency room visits are for things like sprains, minor cuts, etc. These kind of injuries can actually be handled at your nearest urgent care center. The co-pay amount at an urgent care center is going to be much less than what you would pay for a hospital emergency room visit. Don't wait for an emergency to arise. Google "urgent care centers" today and select one in your area. If you ever need medical assistance you will know exactly where to go.

How to save on prescriptions

Ask for a generic.

According to FDA, the cost of a generic version of a drug is on average 80% lower than the name brand drug. You are not using something inferior when you buy a generic. The FDA requires generic drugs to meet the same quality and performance of the name brand. The reason why generics are so much cheaper is because they don't spend billions on advertising generics. Big drug companies tack on the advertising cost to name brand drugs. That's right you the consumer must pay more for a prescription so they can run those silly tv commercials.

Save Money By Splitting Pills

You can save on your prescription when you split certain pills. Pharmacies often charge a similar price for varying doses, For example, a pharmacy might charge $110.00 for 40 Lipitor (Atorvastatin) 10mg tablets and $135.00 for 40 Lipitor 20mg tablets. The patient will save about $40.00 each month by splitting the 20mg Lipitor tablets priced at $135.00.

You will not be able to split certain jells and suspension drugs. Consult with pharmacist or doctor to find out if you can split your prescription pills.

Compare drug store prices

The prices of prescription drugs often vary. Be sure to shop around. Walmart and Costco consistently offer competitive prices on their medications.

Partnership for Prescription Assistance

You may be able to get help with paying for your prescription, through "Partnership for Prescription Assistance". It's a program designed to help patients without prescription drug coverage obtain the medicines they need. If you qualify for the program you can get medication for little or no cost. **To learn more, visit: www.pparx.org**

How to save on dental expenses

Some dental plans are nothing to brag about. They often leave patient with big out of pocket expenses. The best approach is to spread out your dental work so it will extend into the benefits renewal period. If you need $2,500 worth of work and your benefits max out at $1,500, order half the work done now and the other half next year when your benefits reset.

Also, just like with anything you have to comparison shop for dental care. After you get a diagnosis statement from the dentist, contact your insurance provider and ask what contracted rates they have with other dentists for the services you need. The insurance company should provide you with list.

Also, consider using a dental school hospital. They charge nearly half the cost for common procedures. Trained dental staff members closely supervise the work.

Use home remedies to whiten teeth

You don't have to spend money on expensive whitening systems to get that Hollywood smile. You can effectively whiten your teeth by swishing an equal parts mixture of water and hydrogen peroxide in your mouth everyday. This together with twice per day brushing (morning and night) will work wonders.

How to save on College Expenses

The cost of college is soaring like crazy. According to *The College Board*, college tuition and fees will increase by 6% each year. In 18 years the cost of a 4-year private college will reach $340,800 and the cost of public college will reach $95,000. Students will absorb a mountain of student loan debt to pay for college and get a degree, which they hope will lead to great job. Unfortunately, it might take a while to land that dream job in a fierce labor market.

As you know student loans bills don't stop coming during periods of unemployment. So wouldn't it be nice to eliminate or at least slash a student loan?

Well the good news is you can reduce your student loan debt.

Here are some strategies that will work:

Sign up for Upromise

Upromise is a FREE program that allows families to get money back (1% - 25%) for college savings from everyday purchases (online shopping, groceries dining out, almost anything). The cash back earnings can be rolled into a 529 plan savings account.

Also, Upromise is not just a program reserved for parents. It's open to everyone including high school students, current college students, and grads. You can use your cash back earnings to pay student expenses you have now or will owe in the future. You can pay down your Sallie Mae student loans. Also, Upromise offers grocery coupons. You earn cash back when you use the coupons. Upromise is an all-round great way to get help paying for college. To learn more about Upromise, visit www.upromise.com

Community College Option

Students can save up to $20,000 or more by attending community college for 2 years and later transfer to a four-year university. Most universities will accept general education credits from an accredited community college. The savings achieved from 2 years of community college will reduce the total cost of college.

A four-year degree will not be diminished by those 2 years of community college.

University Payment Plan

Many colleges offer a flexible payment plan to students who prefer not to take out student loan and instead pay their tuition out of pocket. By going this route a student will graduate with very little or zero student loan debt. Savings achieved from attending community college and money from part-time job will help cover those payments. The college may add finance charge for the payment plan. The finance charge is actually sometimes lower than interest rate on student loans.

Student Grants and Scholarships

There are so many grants and scholarships frequently overlooked by college bound students. Don't miss out on these funding opportunities. A great resource for finding college money is FoundationCenter.org. This site has the best database of college funding sources. You put in a little info and the site will generate a targeted list of available grants and scholarships. The site does charge a subscription fee but you can use it for free at local library.

Also, parents should encourage kids to get involved with a sports team or student activities group early in high school. This may lead to a college scholarship. It will not hurt to invest money in sports camps and other resources to help a young person tone their skills. Also, a kid doesn't have to be an all-star to get scholarship. The combination of excellent grades and good sportsmanship is sometimes enough to attract the attention of colleges who want student athletes that perform well in the classroom.

How to save on textbooks

Students can save on textbooks due to the migration of textbooks to digital ebooks, which cost up to 75% less than traditional textbooks. It's worth the investment to buy an ebook reader.

The leading ebook readers on the market right now are Amazon Kindle and B&N Nook. You can alternatively download the Kindle or Nook app for free. You will have access to ebooks directly on your pc, mac, iphone, or smartphone. Another way to save is to rent college textbooks. For a coupon code on textbook rentals, visit CouponCodeWorld.com and click on "Campus Deals".

Free College Courses

Several colleges and universities now offer FREE internet based college level courses. The courses available cover a wide range of topics including humanities, social science, computer science, business, and more. Top tier professors from respected schools present these courses online.

Anyone with access to computer may enroll in classes. You do receive recognition for completing courses. It's a wonderful opportunity to learn new skills that will help you reach your personnel and career goals. Obviously the biggest benefit is that it won't cost you one dime to take classes.

To start taking classes for free, visit www.coursera.org, www.edx.org, or udacity.com.

"Cash is King"

You know that old saying "Cash is King". It often rings true at the register. The credit card companies charge merchants a fee when you pay with card. You might qualify for discount on a big-ticket item if you offer to pay cash. Some gas stations even have signage that clearly offers a discount to cash paying customers. But, you typically have to ask a merchant for the cash discount and if you do the answer will frequently be YES. Remember, if you want a discount just ask for it.

How to lower your credit card interest rate

Regularly check your credit report to see where you stand in terms of credit worthiness. You could qualify for a better rate if your score has improved. You have nothing to lose by calling the credit card company and asking for lower rate. Even one tenth of a percentage point drop translates into significant cash savings.

Potential Yearly Savings: $135.00 - $1,250.00+

How to save on mortgage and car payments

Pay extra on your note each month.

You will have money to spare if you consistently follow the tips mentioned in *Extreme Savings*. You could save an incredible amount if you apply that extra money to your note payment.

For Example, lets say you have a 30-year, $225,000 mortgage at 6% interest. By paying an extra:

*$25 Per Month, you could save nearly $15,000 in future interest and pay off the loan 1 year early.

*$100 Per Month, you could save nearly $50,000 in future interest and pay off the loan 4 years early.

*$250 Per Month, you could save nearly $96,000 in future interest and pay off the loan 9 years early.

Remember, The banks charge you to borrow money in the form of interest. But, when you reduce the interest you are essentially getting FREE Money from banks!

To find out how much you'll save on your actual mortgage or car note, Click on the "Extra Payment Calculator" at ExtremeSavingsBook.com

How to file your taxes for FREE

If you have a simple 1040 tax return there really is no need for you to pay for tax preparation services. Plenty of sites including TurboTax.com, TaxAct.com, and FreeTaxUSA.com offer free online tax filing. Also you can contact the IRS directly at 1-800-829-1040 and get FREE tax preparation help and speak with a tax professional about your return.

How to get FREE software

Consumers spend well over 200 billion dollars per year on computer software products. That figure is actually surprising given the fact that you can get everything from anti-virus to photo editing software for absolutely FREE on the internet. Actually some of the free software programs have better user ratings than the ones that cost money. Avira is among the highest rated anti-virus utilities on the planet and it's available free of charge. To get free software for your computer, visit downloads.zdnet.com or download.cnet.com

The vast majority of software downloads on zdnet and cnet are from trusted sources, but there is allot of junk listed as well. Read the user reviews before you download anything to your computer.

Slash your printer ink cost

When you are shopping for printers, pay close attention to price of replacement ink. Ask the sales rep point blank about ink cost. Sometimes a couple of ink replacements will exceed the entire price of the printer itself. You should avoid those types of printers.

Also, print in draft mode using smaller font. A major university recently saved $35,000 by changing to smaller font. Another alternative is to use printer ink refill services such as Cartridge World. To find the lowest prices on printers and printer ink, enter "Printer Ink" in search box at CouponCodeWorld.com

Subscribe to your favorite magazine

You might occasionally buy magizines at the supermarket newsstand. But, you can save money by subscribing to that magazine. For example, a subscription to People magazine sells for nearly 40% off the cover price on Amazon.com. Also, you can read online articles from leading magazines FREE at www.toparticlestoday.com

How to save on morning cup of coffee

Buy a single cup coffer maker.

The Keurig line of coffee makers will give you a cup that rivals what you would buy at Starbucks. Once you have the Keurig you won't be splurging money on that coffee pit stop. Just lock and load your travel cup in Keurig and you will be set. Also, get a My K-cup coffee filter. You can then use bagged ground coffee, which will last longer and is much cheaper than the K-cups.

How to gamble for FREE

The idea of winning that big jackpot is fun. But, the price you have to pay for a chance to win is way too expensive. If you enjoy the thrill of a chance to win cash enter free contests and sweepstakes. They don't take your money and sometimes the odds of winning are actually better. You will not believe what they are giving away for FREE (money, cars, vacations, so much!). To get in on the fun, visit CouponCodeWorld.com and click on "Contests / Sweepstakes) or visit these sites: www.online-sweepstakes.com, www.sweepsadvantage.com, www.contestgirl.com

Fix It Yourself

Avoid costly repair bill by doing preventive upkeep on your appliances. Take a little time to periodically clean your fridge condenser coils (every 12 months) and remove lint from your dryer vents and ducts. Did you know a lint-clogged dryer could consume

$20 worth of extra electricity each month? That's right, it pays to keep your dryer clean!

Also, if you do have trouble with an appliance, first look for a quick fix solution on help site such as eHow.com or Wikihow.com. These sites have thousands of videos and written tutorials on how to fix huge variety of breaks.

Cut back on bottled water

American consumers spend over 14 billion dollars annually on bottled water. This figure is astonishing for a product readily available for free. In fact, most of the "fresh springs" bottled water comes out of a huge faucet not much different from at home.

But, if you like the piece of mine you get from drinking bottled water use a PUR water filter pitcher. It removes impurities from water. They are available at Amazon.com for about twenty dollars. PUR water pitchers yield up to 40 gallons of crisp clean tasting water before you have to change filter. You would have to pay over $150.00 for 40 gallons of the leading brand of bottled water. Also, if you like to bring bottled water to work or outdoor events purchase insulated sports bottles and fill them with water from the PUR pitcher. Potential Yearly Savings: $150.00 - $275.00+

Keep your receipts

You would think that it's common sense to keep receipts, but so many people toss receipts in the bag. If the bag is going in the trash so is the receipt. Tell the cashier to put the receipt in your hand. Stick it in coupon organizer or safe place just for receipts.

If you need to return product and don't have the receipt your money is gone. Don't settle for store credit or exchange. You paid cash for the product so you should get back cash. Also, the price of an item might drop shortly after you buy it, and if that happens you can bring your receipt to the store for price adjustment. A number of retailers including Whole Foods, Nordstrom, Sears and Kmart offer the option to receive a digital copy of your receipt via email. Take advantage of this feature!

Keep receipts for any big ticket purchases such as jewelry, expensive electronics, furniture, etc. Put those receipts in a fire proof safe. You want the receipts to survive fire or other incident for insurance purposes. Snap pictures and record a video of valuable items in your house. This will help serve as proof of ownership if you ever need to file an insurance claim.

Financial Fitness Blueprint

The introduction of *Extreme Savings* states that this book will take you beyond the scope of coupons and how to score great deals when you shop. Now it's time to explore some ways to save money and build your wealth at the same time. The topics discussed are introductory and touch on things such as stocks and investing. It's not intended to be a full-scale investment course.

This is not everyone's favorite cup of tea. If you have no interest in the subjects of investing or money management then feel free to skip this section. But, hopefully you will find the information enlightening. At the end of the section there are resources that you can utilize to learn more about the topics discussed. Please remember this material is offered only for informational purposes. It should not be considered as investment advice. Consult with an investment professional before you invest.

Where is your money?

The first step to take toward improving your finances is to simply focus on where you keep your money...The Bank.

Are you paying unnecessary fees for your account?

Banks make big money on service fees, which is why they will offer you an account with monthly service fees the minute you walk into branch. If you are paying a monthly service fee, request free checking or savings account. If they don't offer it move your money to another bank.

How to get FREE money from banks

Several banks including Chase and CapitalOne 360 routinely offer coupon codes you can use to get FREE money when you open a new account. All you have to do is mention the coupon code when you open your new account. You can even open it online within minutes. To find the latest bank account coupon codes, click on "Free Money" at CouponCodeWorld.com.

How to avoid ATM and overdraft fees

When you need pocket cash look for your own bank's atm. If you can't find a branch atm nearby, visit drugstore like Walgreens or CVS/Pharmacy and get cash back at the register. You could buy a pack of gum or something. They will give you cash back with no fees if you use your debit card.

Drop any overdraft protection on your account. Instead link your checking account to your savings account to avoid overdraft fees. By doing so the bank will automatically transfer from your savings to checking account if you are overdrawn. This beats paying that $35.00 overdraft fee. Another good idea is to sign-up for text alerts from your bank that notify you when your bank balance is low.

Also, you can order personal checks on the Internet at fraction of the cost banks charge. For cheap checks, visit these sites: www.checks.com, www.checksunlimited.com, or www.vistaprint.com

How to get FREE money from your job

If your employer offers 401(k) program enroll the very first day you are eligible to participate. Under 401(k) plan you are allowed to contribute a portion of your income to a 401(k) savings account. It's a portfolio of stocks, bonds, and mutual funds. The best advantage of a 401 (k) is that your job may contribute matching funds to the account.

For example, an employer might contribute $3.00 for every $1.00 the employee put into the 401(k) account up to certain amount. Another big perk is that the money comes out of income before taxes are deducted. So you'll pay less in taxes because the contribution reduces your total taxable income. Also, the money in your 401(k) is allowed to grow tax deferred until you are eligible to withdraw the funds at age 59.

But, don't even think about withdrawing from your 401(k) prior to age 59. You will get hit with a huge tax penalty if you do it.

Remember, sign-up the very first day of eligibility to participate in your employer 401(k) plan. It's Free Money that will grow fast!

Adjust your federal tax withholding

The average IRS tax refund is $2,400, which means $200.00 or more in excess taxes are withheld from paychecks of Americans every month. You may enjoy getting that tax refund at the end of the year, but it's not a gift from the government. It's actually repayment for an interest free loan you give Uncle Sam each year.

Why should you loan the government money? Ask your employer to adjust the number of allowances on your w4 form. You could put that extra money into a 401(k) or mutual fund. For example, if you deposit $200.00 each month into an account earning 10% you would have $15,000 within 5 years.

How to never pay late fees

The reason why so many people miss payment due dates has nothing to do with not being able to pay their bills. It's because people don't mail off their payment on time. You will steer clear of this problem by using online bill payment. Banks typically offer online bill payment free of charge to customers. You might even get a cash bonus from your bank when you sign-up. Take a day out of every month to get on the computer and pay all of your monthly bills at once. Also, some credit card companies will remove late or overdraft fee onetime as a courtesy if you request to have fee removed. Potential Yearly Savings: $75.00 - $450.00+

How to CONTROL your money

If you don't keep track of where every last penny of your paycheck is spent you are NOT in control of your money. Take control by using financial management software. These software programs allow you to manage expenses and see exactly what is going in and out of your bank account.

You will be able to easily identify and eliminate wasteful spending. Some of the leading Financial Management Software programs include: Quicken, Mint.com (FREE), and Youneedabudget.com

To access debt freedom calculator, click on "Debt Help Resources" at ExtremeSavingsBook.com

How to become a millionaire!

The easiest way to become a millionaire in your lifetime is to take all the savings you achieve from consistently using the tips and strategies in this book. Put that money into solid long-term investment account. All the coupon savings and discounts on everything from groceries to movie rentals will result in you having a continual stream of money to invest.

Plant your Million Dollar Money Tree

When you use a product coupon it's like that company has given you a little seed for your Million Dollar Money Tree. The goal is for your tree to eventually grow into 1 million dollars or more. Let's say that you save $100.00 per month by just using coupons alone. You deposit this money directly into the investment account you have for your nest egg. Look at your potential earnings:

*If you deposit $100.00 from coupon savings into your investment account (Assuming 19% Return Rate), it will grow to $10,000 after 5 yrs and eventually grow to the following amounts:

After 15 years: $55,000.00

After 20 years: $271,000.00

After 27 years: $1 Million Dollars

After 30 years: $1.8 Million Dollars

How to earn 1 million dollars faster?

The above example assumes you are depositing $100.00 into your account. But, you should realize after reading *Extreme Savings* that you will save well over $100 per month if use only a fraction of the tips in this book. So that means you could actually invest more money. You will reach that million-dollar mark 7-10 years faster if you deposit more money in your investment account. Let's say you put aside $350.00 instead of $100.00 each month. Again look at your potential earnings:

After just 5 years: $35,000.00

After 20 years: $1 Million Dollars

After 27 years: $3 Million Dollars

After 30 years: $6 Million Dollars

The above figures are based on an investment account that is consistently generating 19% return. So where can you find an investment account that will yield a 19% return? Well if you do a little homework and visit www.Morningstar.com (Click on Tools – Mutual Fund Leaders") you'll find some very attractive investment opportunities with solid returns. Here are a few funds to consider:

UBS Bloomberg CMCI Silver Total Return index (Symbol: USV)
*Return Avg: 43.05% (3 Years)

iShares Gold Trust (Symbol: IAU)
*Return Avg: 29.54% (3 years)

ICON Energy (Symbol: ICENX)
*Return Avg: 21.09% (10 Years)

USAA Precious Metals and Minerals
(Symbol: USAGX)
*Return Avg: 19.39% (10 Years)

BlackRock Global Resources Inv A
(Symbol: SSGRX)
*Return Avg: 19.24% (10 Years)

If you would have bought 300 shares of the silver index stock (USV) when it was at $13.20 per share (11/2008) that $4,600 investment would have grown to $20,000 based on (USV) price of $60.00 per share (09/2011). You can still capitalize on (USV) because the stock has some room to climb.

But, you might want to consider stock that is currently low and trending upward such as iShares Gold Trust (Symbol: IAU). The price of iShares Gold Trust as of (08/2013) is around $16.00 per share. It's currently trading on the low end because of a 10-1 split on June 24, 2010. But, if you check the historical prices of iShares Gold Trust you'll notice that the stock was priced at high of $119.00 per share on June 1, 2010.

Would you buy a bar of gold regular priced $119.00 marked down to $16.00 at the supermarket? If your answer is YES, then you should consider buying iShares Gold Trust stock (Symbol: IAU).

To learn more about above stocks, enter symbol into "Get Quote" search box at scotttrade.com or your favorite online trading site.

Now even if you are currently earning a 1% - 5% return on your money you can still reach that million-dollar mark. You'll simply need to invest more of the money you have garnered from using the savings strategies highlighted in this book.

The overall point here is that if you don't have an investment plan you should establish one and start putting money away NOW so you can get on the path to wealth and financial freedom.

Stock Pricing Info Based on Yahoo Finance Historical Data

How to buy stocks the easy way

You don't really need to hire an investment adviser to buy or sell stocks. Online trading sites have made it super easy for people to buy stocks, mutual funds, and other investment products on computer. You just sign up for a trading account, which is free to do at several online trading sites. After you sign-up, you can fund your account with as little as $100 and start trading!

You will feel a sense of prestige when you buy stocks. If you buy Walmart stock (WMT), you will shop at a place that you partially own. When Walmart makes money, you make money too. Cool!

That's Awesome!

Here's an example of how you can make money trading stocks: Let say, you have an extra $400.00 in disposable income thanks to couponing and your other penny pitching habits. So you decide to head over to sharebuilder.com and buy some stocks. You might be enjoying a cold glass of Dean's Milk when you realize how much you like it and decide to do some research on Dean Foods stock (Symbol: DF). Everything looks good. It's a reputable company flushed with cash not on the verge of bankruptcy. So you buy 50 shares at $8.00 per share. You sit back relax and check on the stock from time to time. You notice one day that the stock price has increased to $19.99 per share.

Well at that point your initial $400.00 investment has more than doubled to $1,000 in value. You hit the sell button on your computer and abracadabra you've got $1,000 in your account. So in a nutshell it's all about buying low and selling high with some technical jargon in between.

Of course there is risk involved when you invest in stocks. Things don't always turn out rosy as illustrated in the prior example. The Dean Food stock prices mentioned are actually real historical prices of the stock. But, it's possible that the stock might go down not up after you buy it. You can indeed lose money.

The stock market can be volatile at times, but it has consistently generated positive return for investors in the long run.

What stocks should you buy?

A good way to choose stocks is to first consider companies that make the products you believe in and enjoy using. If you drive a Ford, do some research on Ford stocks (Symbol: F).

If you love your iPhone or iPod look into Apple (Symbol: AAPL).

You can rely on the same tactics you use to score deals at the supermarket when shopping for stocks. You want to buy stocks when they are priced as low as possible just like you do with grocery items. For example, Ford stock was priced at $1.91 back in February of 2009. If you had purchased 500 shares of Ford in 2009 and sold them at going price of $16.51 in February of 2011 you would have netted about $7,300. Not Bad!

There will always be bargain stocks available that could potential pay off big time for you later. But, you won't accomplish anything by sitting on the sidelines thinking about "what ifs". You must get in the game and start playing with REAL money!

Stock trading is an exciting activity that millions of people like you enjoy at home on their computer. You have good chance of doing well if you utilize the great research tools provided by the various online trading sites. Also, join an investment club or start one with your friends. You'll gain a great support group that will give you access to investment tips and advice helping you succeed. Also, many of the online trading sites will pay you a referral fee when you refer friends. That's Free Money!

Online Investing Websites: www.tdameritrade.com, www.sharebuilder.com, www.scottrade.com

If you prefer to use a broker or investment advisor, be sure to periodically check their credentials at www.nasaa.org or contact FINRA at 1 (800) 289-9999.

Also, request stock certificates from your broker for any substantial holdings. This will help verify that no funny business is going on and that you actually own stock. By law they are required to honor your request. Details on the certificate itself will be your name, the company's name and the number of shares you own.

Never put all of your eggs into one single stock regardless of the good things you've heard about it. You should diversify and spread out your investment among several stocks with history of paying out dividends. ETFs (Exchange Traded Funds) are popular among investors. A leading ETF is the Dow Industrial Average (Symbol: DIA), which is a fund comprised of several leading blue chip stocks. When you buy one ETF stock you are investing in the top 30 blue chip companies. The fund consistently yields a 2% - 3% return and ongoing dividends.

Don't wait one day longer

Hopefully you have already taken measures to secure your financial future either through a 401k plan or another investment strategy. But, if you are not on that path you need to commit TODAY to the following four things:

1. Live within your means
2. Save a fixed amount of money each month.
3. Set goals for growth of your money.
4. Invest your money in diverse portfolio of stocks, bonds, or alternative investments such as real estate or a small business venture that will help you attain your financial goals.

According to report by the Deloite Center for Financial Services, the number of millionaires in the US is projected to more than double to 20.5 million by 2020. You could be one of them as long as you stay on course with your investment strategy.

Additional Investing Resources

To learn more specifics about stocks and other growth investments review the following resources available at Amazon.com:

Investing Online For Dummies (Matt Krantz)

How to Get Started in Stocks (Paul Larson)

All About Index Funds: The Easy Way to Get Started (Richard Ferri)

*The information provided in this section should not be perceived as investment advice and it's only provided for informational purposes.

How to eliminate debt faster

Nearly every person on earth desires to grow that million-dollar money tree mention in the previous section. Unfortunately, suffocating debt leaves little or no room for many families to save money for retirement.

The average US credit card debt per household is staggering $16,000. This kind of debt has the potential to completely dismantle a person's credit report, which is critical to getting many of the things needed in life. A poor credit report and old debts could cost you a job, new home, or make it hard to get a loan.

Here are some tips to improve your credit and help you get out of debt so you can truly get on the path to financial freedom:

Try to avoid looking risky

All of your credit card transactions are monitored and feed into a computer that measures how risky you are as a borrower. This level of risk in turn determines your credit score. Certain behaviors make you appear more risky lowering your credit score.

Here are things to avoid:

Credit Card Cash Advances

Frequent cash advances indicate that you are suddenly desperate for money due to job loss or being underemployed. You don't appear able to repay loan so lenders won't bother with you. Also, the cash advance amount will be added to your credit card balance, resulting in less available credit. This will undoubtedly hurt your credit score. Avoid getting cash advances.

Minimum Payments

The credit card companies want you to carry balance so they can make money from interest. But, other lenders will see on your credit report that you just pay the minimum giving the impression that you are struggling to make payments and can't afford another loan. Also, your credit card balance will never really go down if you only make the minimum payment. Your credit card balance impacts FICO score, so you must pay more than the minimum to reduce credit card balance. Your FICO score will gradually rise when your credit card balance decreases. Also, you look like a person in good financial shape if you pay more than the minimum or better yet pay off your balance entirely each month.

Other Person's Debt

When you co-sign to help some one-else get a loan, you're credit will be affected regardless if the person pays back that loan. Why? Because the debt is added to your credit report. You look more risky with extra debt on your shoulders.

Excessive Credit Inquires

Whenever you apply for new credit it appears as an inquiry on your report. If you apply for 2 or 3 credit cards within short period of time the FICO scoring system will flag this as indication that you are in financial trouble seeking more credit for survival.

House Short Sale

People are often told that a "short sale" will not hurt their credit report. But, according to recent statement by Experian's Public Education Department, a short sale is reported as "settled amount" lesser than what was originally owed on house and that "settled status" is equally negative as a foreclosure. One way to lessen the impact of a short sale on your credit report is to directly request during negotiations that the lender not report difference between the short sale amount and actual mortgage amount as "balance owed" to the credit bureaus.

Get a copy of your credit report

You have to be aware of what's on your credit report by closely monitoring it. People may not give their credit a second thought until one day they want to make that big purchase only to find out they have low credit scores. Knowledge is the key. Credit scores range from 350 to 850, the higher your score, the more buying power you have. You need a maintain a minimum credit score of 610 in order to qualify for loans and credit cards with a decent interest rate. For people who have credit issues, the first thing to do is obtain a credit report from all three credit bureaus. You are entitled to one free credit report every year. You can request this by visiting www.annualcreditreport.com. Don't let other similar sites fool you. They merely want you to sign up for a monthly monitoring service. This is not a bad option, but keep in mind you are entitled to one free credit report every year. This should help you stay on top of any inaccuracies that might occur.

How to fix your credit report

A Federal Trade Commission study revealed that one in five consumers have errors on their credit report. That means there is a 20% chance something is wrong on your credit report. These mistakes could seriously damage your ability to get a loan with decent terms or find a job. Remember employers, lenders, insurance companies all look at credit.

For inaccuracies on your credit report, you can write a letter to the credit bureau reporting the inaccuracy and request the information be corrected. Make sure you have the documentation such as paid in full letters or receipts. Mail the letters by registered mail with return receipt so you have proof it was received and by who. Make sure to have your name, date of birth, social security number and reference the item in question. The credit bureau has 30 days to investigate and update your credit report if it is indeed an inaccuracy. If the information is indeed proven to be wrong, the credit bureaus will send you a response letter and remove it. If they don't correct the mistake then contact your state attorney general or speak with a consumer law attorney. For assistance visit www.naca.net (National Association of Consumer Advocates)

I've cleared up my credit, now what happens?

When you have all inaccurate information on your credit cleaned up and removed, it is crucial to make all payments on time. When trying to obtain a mortgage, lenders look for a minimum of 12 months of all bills being paid on time. If you can make more than the required minimum monthly payment, this will help to increase your credit scores. Keep no more than four credit cards open and don't overcharge them. The potential to charge more is much greater if you have more than four credit cards.

Again, you want to show creditors that you are disciplined. When your credit scores increase you now have buying power and are in charge of your life and future.

How to improve credit

Prioritize your debt obligations

Make a column for necessary bills versus unnecessary ones. Of course your housing and utilities are priority. What might not be priority are credit card bills or unpaid medical bills leftover from insurance. You can always make small payments on medical bills and as long as you are making some kind of effort, they will not turn it over to collection agencies. They are typically very willing to work with you. Consistently making your payments on time will prevent any additional negative reporting and help your credit rating keep from falling.

Budgeting is another key factor to repairing credit. You need to write down everything you spend and go over critical versus non-critical bills. Obviously you're rent or house payment, food, utilities are critical. Credit cards would be non-critical. If you budget your money and spend wisely, you are more likely to be able to pay all of your bills on time, which is going to improve your credit over time. If you write down everything you spend money on, you'll be surprised by how much you are actually spending on items that are not necessary.

Saving money can be achieved by cutting down on your bills and should be achievable if you are on a budget. Set aside portion of your pay or have it automatically transferred to your savings account. If you never have it to begin with, you won't miss it. This will build up over time and if a down payment is ever needed for a purchase, you will have it. It's always a good to have a cushion.

Cut back on that dinner out and enjoy cooking at home, skip that extra coffee in the morning. You will be surprised at how much money over time it will add up to. It's simple to cut back on the little things that just aren't necessary. Have you ever heard the saying, "save it for a rainy day"? If an emergency comes up and you don't have a savings to fall back on, you will fall behind on some bills, which are going to negatively affect your credit that you have been working so hard to improve.

What to do if you have no established credit?

If lack of credit is the issue, there are credit card companies that will issue secure credit cards, or even unsecured with low credit limits, to those with low credit scores, or no score at all (someone who has never established any credit). The key is to only charge 25% of what your limit is. For example, if your limit is $100, you will want to charge $25, but no more. This shows credit grantors that you are responsible. Also, you never want to close an account as this can reflect negatively on you. The best thing to do if you don't want to carry a balance is to just leave it open with a zero balance. To find a secured credit card, visit: www.bankrate.com

What happens if you fall behind on your payments?

If you are no longer able to make minimum payments on accounts such as credit cards, car payments, you will first be recorded late for every 30 days you fall behind. The further you fall behind, the lower it brings your credit scores. One 30 day late for instance won't affect your score near as much as a 60 or 90 day late or several of them. A pattern of many repeated late payments lower your score to the point of not having any buying power at all.

If you can no longer make your payments, you can call the company and ask if they will settle on an amount less than your total balance. They would rather settle than continue to not receive any money at all. For instance if you owe $2000, they may settle the debt entirely for $1000 or maybe even less. This is a good alternative to filing a bankruptcy, which will more adversely affect your credit and ability to obtain loans or mortgages in the future. You will need to ensure that you have the cash on hand when requesting to settle on a debt. You can achieve this by budgeting and saving as previously discussed. Settling your debts is very important if you ever want to make a large purchase such as buying your first home or that car you've always wanted.

When calling to settle a debt, get everything in writing. Always take down the name and phone number of the person you speak with.

What you should know about Debt Collections

Here are things to remember about debt collection accounts:

Federal law requires credit-reporting bureaus to remove negative accounts after seven years. The debt clock starts turning 180 days after the first missed payment.

The creditor is not allowed to restart the seven-year clock by assigning a new delinquency date to the account (re-aging) or selling the account to a different agency.

The Fair Debt Collection Practices Act prohibits a creditor to sue or even threaten to sue you after the statue of limitations have run out on a debt collection. The creditor only is allowed a certain time period to sue you over a debt, which is 2-6 years in most States.

Don't allow a creditor to sue in a State with a longer statue of limitations if that State is not your current place of residence or where you entered into the agreement.

Don't agree to make any new payment arrangements on an outstanding account, because it may re-start the seven-year clock.

If you believe that a debt is too old, mail a letter to all three credit bureaus (Equifax, Experian, TransUnion) stating that the statue of limitations has expired and you want it removed from your credit report. Also, send a duplicate letter to the creditor.

A debt will exist until it is settled or paid in full regardless of statute of limitations. The creditor can continue to send collection letters and make calls.

They are not allowed to call prior to 8:00 a.m. or after 9:00 p.m.

They cannot call you at your place of work if you advise them you are not allowed to accept personal phone calls.

They cannot threaten you or make promises they will not keep.

You can file a lawsuit and may be eligible to receive compensation if a debt collector or credit bureau violates your consumer rights.

To file a complaint, contact an attorney or call the Federal Trade Commission (FTC) at 1 (877) 382-4357.

About Debt Settlement Companies

Be leery of companies that say they can erase all negative debt on your credit report. What they can do is get your balance settled for a lesser amount, which is nothing more than you can do yourself. They charge a fee for this service and they do no more than make the phone calls you can make and request that the amount be settled. They will sometimes consolidate your bills and charge a monthly fee to disperse the payments to your creditors.

You are better off keeping your money in your bank account and calling each creditor to ask if they will work with you to either settle or possibly waive or defer a payment to help you get caught up. You'll find that most creditors are more than willing to help you work things out. If you follow the steps mentioned in this section, you will be able to settle your own debts and save money. There are sample debt settlement letters at the end of this section.

Fill in your information on the letters and start mailing and faxing them to debt collectors immediately. You can initially offer to pay 20 - 30% of the original past due balance, which is basally a starting point in negotiations. The debt collector could accept initial offer thus clearing your debt or they might make a counteroffer slightly above your offer. Even if the debtor doesn't accept your initial offer the counter offer could be around 50% of original debt and that beats paying the full amount.

Take care of your credit

Unfortunately people don't realize the value of good credit until they try to make a purchase and can't. Even to get auto insurance, a credit report can be pulled. A credit report with low scores will mean higher insurance premiums. Poor credit can also keep someone from landing that job they want. Poor credit will also mean when you do obtain a loan or a mortgage, you will pay a higher interest rate because of it. It's never too late to work on repairing your credit.

Stay clear from those who promise to clean up your credit for a fee. They can't do anything that you can't do yourself. It may take some time to write those letters to the credit bureaus and send receipts of things paid, etc, but it's worth the investment of time.

There are resources to help you. The FTC offers free tools to help consumers maintain good credit. For free information and assistance, visit www.ftc.gov.

Be sure to take a look at other helpful resources and sample debt resolution letters in the back of this book.

Ready To Roll?

The goal of *Extreme Savings* is to provide you with fundamental information that will help you get on the path to financial freedom.

Hopefully you have been enlightened about the broad horizon of ways to save money. It's not easy for everyone to save money in an environment that revolves around spending money.

Companies run multi-billion dollar marketing machine designed to influence you to buy their products. They advertise during your favorite tv shows and radio programs. They use Facebook to get in your face as often as possible. They use services like Groupon to get in your email. It's a huge well tuned machine that runs 24/7 in effort to do one primary thing...CONTROL YOUR MONEY and guess what? It works. That's why all of the coupons and Groupons will keep coming.

Do you think they are offering those irresistible half-off deals just to be nice and help you save money? NO.

They are doing it to make you open your wallet and spend money like there is no tomorrow. This is not intended to suggest that you don't take advantage of coupon deals or free offers. In fact you should exploit those deals whenever possible.

But remember that these companies are eager to secure their own prosperity at your expense. When you understand the whole idea behind their tactics you will beat them at their own game.

It's about YOU!

Take care of yourself NOT the companies out to get your money. Do everything necessary to secure your own financial future. Deposit at least 15% of your paycheck into a safe retirement account. Also, remember these two things:

1. The unexpected could happen at any moment without warning.

2. The unexpected will turn a comfortable life upside down.

Keep enough money in emergency fund to cover your expenses 3-6 months in case an unexpected event occurs such as a job loss, sudden medical emergency, etc. If you have no emergency fund, start one right now. Set up a separate bank account with fixed amount automatically going into the account. It will eventually grow to the necessary level. Don't touch the money unless there is a real emergency. After you've established an emergency fund, focus on your revolving debts (credit cards, car note, student loans, mortgage payment, etc.).

Debt Freedom Steps

1. Pay off every single credit card. Start with the lowest balance card and then work your way up to highest balance credit card.

2. After you tackle your high interest credit cards, move onto other debt such as car note or student loan (whichever has the next lowest balance). Add a little extra to your payment or if possible pay off the entire balance.

3. Last but not least, eliminate mortgage payment. Pay off your mortgage as soon as possible. You learned in *Financial Fitness* section about how adding a little extra to your payment each month will enable you to pay your mortgage faster.

Where do you get money to put toward debts?

If you consistently utilize the numerous savings tips and strategies discussed in *Extreme Savings*, you will find yourself with extra money to put toward your debts. Here are some other ways to bring in more income:

- Ask for additional hours at your job.

- Perhaps start a small business. There are hundreds of business opportunities available that don't require a huge investment. The right small businesses could help generate significant income for you. To find small business opportunities, visit www.sbomag.com or refer to "Additional Resources" section.

- Freelance and part-time gigs. To find work google "freelance jobs" or visit these websites: freelancer.com, gigwalk.com, odesk.com, worknine.com

- Sell any items collecting dust around your house. You could get cash for things you don't want or no longer use such as furniture, clothing, gadgets, etc. Hold a big yard sale or sell your stuff on amazon, ebay, or craigslist.

Use profits and extra income that you earn from above methods to pay down your debts. The sooner you get rid of your debts the sooner you will LIVE FREE!

Hey, Enjoy Life

After you secure your savings and investment accounts then by all means have some fun with your money. Splurge on whatever makes you happy. That's perfectly fine as long as you don't spend beyond the limits of your budget plan. But, please avoid the temptation of using credit to finance your comfort purchases.

Whenever possible pay for things with cash NOT credit. Yes, credit is convenient and useful at times. However, credit also leads to more debt. Remember that debt is the ENEMY. Avoid accumulating debt at all cost. Don't allow anything to stop you from reaching your goals.

"If you've got a dollar and you spend 29 cents on a loaf of bread, you've got 71 cents left; But if you've got seventeen grand and you spend 29 cents on a loaf of bread, you've still got seventeen grand. There's a math lesson for you." - Steve Martin

Thank you for choosing to read *Extreme Savings*. Please tell your friends about *Extreme Savings*. For money-saving tips and freebies, follow CouponCodeWorld.com on Facebook and Twitter.

Review Request

If you enjoyed this book, please take a moment to post a positive review on the book's Amazon Page. You will notice a button that says "Write a customer review" - Just click on it and you're all set.

Thanks for your support!

Additional Resources

Suggested Reading Materials:
(Available at Amazon.com)

Make Money Online - 97 Real Companies That Pay You To Work In Your Pajamas - Connie Brentford

A Beginner's Guide to Investing: How to Grow Your Money the Smart and Easy Way
Ivy Bytes (Author)

The ABCs of Real Estate Investing
Ken McElroy (Author)

Meals Under $10 - 51 Delicious Meals That Won't Break The Bank
Joan Johnson (Author)

Statue of Limitations for Debts

(Note: This is presented for informational purposes and should not be deemed as legal advice.)

Alabama: 3 years
Alaska: 6 years
Arizona: 3 years
Arkansas: 3 years
California: 4 years
Colorado: 6 years
Connecticut: 6 years
Delaware: 3 years
District of Columbia: 3 years
Florida: 4 years
Georgia: 4 years
Hawaii: 6 years
Idaho: 4 years
Illinois: 5 years
Indiana: 6 years
Iowa: 5 years
Kansas: 3 years
Kentucky: 5 years
Louisiana: 3 years
Maine: 6 years
Maryland: 3 years
Massachusetts: 6 years
Michigan: 6 years
Minnesota: 6 years
Mississippi: 3 years
Missouri: 5 years
Montana: 5 years
Nebraska: 4 years
Nevada: 4 years
New Hampshire: 3 years
New Jersey: 6 years
New Mexico: 4 years
New York: 6 years
North Carolina: 3 years
North Dakota: 6 years
Ohio: 6 years
Oklahoma: 3 years

Oregon: 6 years
Pennsylvania: 6 years
Rhode Island: 10 years
South Carolina: 3 years
South Dakota: 6 years
Tennessee: 6 years
Texas: 4 years
Utah: 4 years
Vermont: 6 years
Virginia: 3 years
Washington: 3 years
West Virginia: 5 years
Wisconsin: 6 years
Wyoming: 8 years

Sample Debt Dispute Letters

Use the following sample Debt Dispute Letters to successfully dispute debts after collectors call demanding payment on invalid or expired debts, or to set up payment agreements with creditors.

Sample Debt Collection Dispute Letter

Today's Date

Your Name
Your Address

Collector's Name
Collector's Address

Dear {insert name of collector or company},

I am writing in response to your (letter or phone call) dated {insert date}, (copy enclosed) because I do not believe I owe what you say I owe. This is the first I've heard from you, or any other company on this matter therefore, in accordance with the Fair Debt Collection Practices Act, Section 809(b): Validating Debts:

I respectfully request that you provide me with the following information:

(1) the amount of the debt;
(2) the name of the creditor to whom the debt is owed;
(3) Provide a verification or copy of any judgment (if applicable);
(4) Proof that you are licensed to collect debts in (insert name of your state)

Be advised that I am fully aware of my rights under the Fair Debt Collection Practices Act and the Fair Credit Reporting Act. For instance, I know that because I have disputed this debt in writing within 30 days of receipt of your dunning notice, you must obtain verification of the debt or a copy of the judgment against me and mail these items to me at your expense; you cannot add interest or fees except those allowed by the original contract or state law. You do not have to respond to this dispute but if you do, any attempt to collect this debt without validating it, violates the FDCPA; also be advised that I am keeping very accurate records of all correspondence from you and your company including recording all phone calls and I will not hesitate to report violations of the law to my State Attorney General, the Federal Trade Commission and the Better Business Bureau.

I have disputed this debt; therefore, until validated you know your information concerning this debt is inaccurate. Thus, if you have already reported this debt to any credit-reporting agency (CRA) or Credit Bureau (CB) then, you must immediately inform them of my dispute with this debt. Reporting information that you know to be inaccurate or failing to report information correctly violates the Fair Credit Reporting Act § 1681s-2. Should you pursue a judgment without validating this debt, I will inform the judge and request the case be dismissed based on your failure to comply with the FDCPA.

Finally, if you do not own this debt, I demand that you immediately send a copy of this dispute letter to the original creditor so they are also aware of my dispute with this debt.

Signature here
Your Printed Name

Sample Credit Report Dispute Letter

Date

Your Name
Your Address
City, State Zip
SSN#:

Credit Bureau
Bureau Address
City, State Zip

Dear Credit Bureau,

This letter is a formal complaint that you are reporting inaccurate credit information.

I am very distressed that you have included the below information in my credit profile due to its damaging effects on my good credit standing. As you are no doubt aware, credit-reporting laws ensure that bureaus report only accurate credit information. No doubt the inclusion of this inaccurate information is a mistake on either your or the reporting creditor's part. Because of the mistakes on my credit report, I have been wrongfully denied credit recently for a <insert credit type for which you were denied here>, which was highly embarrassing and has negatively, impacted my lifestyle. With the proof I'm attaching to this letter, I'm sure you'll agree it needs to be removed ASAP.

The following information therefore needs to be verified and deleted from the report as soon as possible:

CREDITOR AGENCY, acct. 123-34567-XXX
Please delete the above information as quickly as possible.

Sincerely,

Your Signature
Your Name
SSN# 123-45-6789
Attachment included

Sample Debt Settlement Offer Letter

SEND VIA CERTIFIED MAIL RRR # (PUT THE NUMBER OF THE CERTIFIED MAIL RECEIPT HERE)

YOUR NAME
YOUR ADDRESS
CITY, STATE, ZIP CODE

Today's Date

Place collector's name here
Collectors address
Collectors city, state, zip

RE: Acct.# 5555554441

Dear (who ever you spoke with):

As we discussed, I was unable to pay on my account due to (example: income loss, family hardship, unexpected expense or illness). As a result, the above-mentioned account was sent to collections (or charged off) by your company.

I would like to either resume payments on this account at $(however much) per month, or settle the balance on this account for $(however much).

I recently obtained a copy of my credit report and noted that your company has reported this account as: (delinquent, sent to collections). I wish to bring this account or matter to a resolution that will be fair, and beneficial for both of us. I hereby propose to pay you: X monthly payments of $money, or remit a check to you in the amount of $debt as payment in full provided you are willing to send me a letter stating you will report this to any and all credit reporting agencies as: 'PAID AS AGREED' or notify me in writing that you agree to delete this item from any and all credit reporting agencies.

Due to the inequities of the system I AM NOT agreeable to accepting a 'PAID P & L' or 'CHARGE OFF' for an additional amount of time on my credit report. It is my position that I have suffered enough as a result of this problem. Upon receipt of your letter I will forward you a cashier's check or money order in the amount of (Agreed $$$).

Yours Truly,
Your signature Today's date signed

Store Coupon Policies
(Based on information provided by retailers)

Albertsons

Albertsons promotes a coupon friendly shopping experience and encourages customers to participate in store, manufacturer and internet coupon use. The following policy guidelines are current, but Albertsons may change this policy at any time and policy changes may not be advertised. Coupon redemptions are subject to the policy in effect at time of redemption. The current policy information can be discussed with individual store management but is not posted in each store.

Coupons – Definition: Coupons are a form of tender to reduce an order total based on merchandise purchased.
Retailers are not required by law to accept manufacturers' coupon.
Coupons can be in print and/or in electronic form, and may be integrated into the register systems where they are deducted automatically when all purchase requirements are met.

General Coupon Acceptance Guidelines

Coupons are accepted in accordance to the stated requirements on the coupon at the time of purchase.
These requirements include, but are not limited to: product type, flavor(s), size(s), quantities and
minimum/maximum dollar purchase limits.
Coupons are intended for one time use and cannot be redeemed more than once. Coupons have no cash value.

Albertsons only accepts original coupons and does not accept photocopied or reproduced coupons (including
multiple prints of same series internet coupons).

Albertsons does not accept expired coupons. Printed expiration dates are verified in addition to scanning the
coupon for validity.

Coupons stating "on next/future purchase or visit" cannot be used in the transaction in which they are
generated. Next purchase is defined as a separate transaction.

The coupon redemption value on 'Free' coupons may not exceed the value of the item.

Albertsons will accept ONE manufacturer coupon and ONE store coupon on the same qualifying item.

Albertsons does not accept competitor coupons. (Coupons generated by any competitor with competitor logo are considered competitor coupons.)

All applicable sales taxes are paid by the customer at the full value of the item.

Albertsons reserves the right to refuse any coupons at its discretion.

Manufacturer Coupons

Coupons issued by manufacturers contain redemption guidelines including, but not limited to: "terms of agreement", "face value", "expiration date" and the verbiage "manufacturer coupon". Albertsons adheres to all manufacturer redemption guidelines.

Albertsons may issue private promotion "manufacturer coupons" in advertisements that state "redeemable only at Albertsons" in which Albertsons is the only retailer that will accept.

Coupons that exceed the retail value of an item will be adjusted to provide the maximum value, not exceeding the price of the item Albertsons accepts internet generated manufacturer coupons that have the following conditions:

Coupons must scan at checkout.

Coupons must have serial numbers and follow an industry-standard format.

Coupons must clearly indicate that they are a manufacturer coupon and have a valid manufacture address on the printed coupon.

Albertsons does not accept internet generated manufacturer coupons that have the following conditions:

FREE product without a required purchase.

A redemption value that exceeds $5.00.

The absence of a clear and scannable UPC bar code.

Albertsons Web Facing Coupon Acceptance Policy:

Albertsons will not accept internet coupons with same serial numbers (internet sites print time & date stamps on coupons and limit the number of coupons that can be printed from same computer). Albertsons will not accept internet coupons with the absence of a valid manufacturer address on the printed coupon.

Store Coupons

Rain checks for store coupons will be given out as long as the store coupon does not state on it "while
supplies last".

Coupons issued by Albertsons contain redemption guidelines including, but not limited to: "terms of
agreement", "face value", "expiration date" and the verbiage "store coupon".

Albertsons offers store coupons in various forms of media including, but not limited to, print, electronic,
newspaper, direct mailers, kiosks and Company websites. Albertsons may issue "store coupons" in advertisements that state "redeemable only at Albertsons" in which Albertsons is the only retailer that will accept. Store coupons may require that the discount applies only with Preferred/Loyalty/Rewards Card use. Twice the Value store coupons can only be used in combination with a $1.00 or less manufacturer coupon (a printed face value of $1.01 or greater cannot be combined with Twice the Value store coupons).

Albertsons DOES allow manufacturer coupons that state they cannot be 'doubled' to be used in
conjunction with a Twice the Value store coupon.

BJ's Wholesale Club

BJ's accepts all manufacturers' coupons including the ones that come in your Sunday newspaper giving you additional savings on top of our everyday low prices.

What are the guidelines for using more than one coupon?

When purchasing a multi-pack of "individual for sale" packaged items, which is a set of items that could be sold individually (each item has a barcode) shrink-wrapped and sold together, Members can combine one BJ's-issued coupon with manufacturers' coupons. However, you cannot exceed the actual retail price in the total value of coupons.

In terms of manufacturers' coupons that are "buy one, get one free," we will honor the coupon for items in stock as long as our price does not exceed the maximum value stated on the coupon. If the manufacturer's coupon does not state the maximum value, we cannot honor the coupon. We cannot accept multiple BJ's-issued coupons on a product.

CVS/Pharmacy

CVS/Pharmacy registers are set to allow 1 CVS coupon and 1 manufacturer coupon per item. Free coupons or "offers at the register" (OAR's) are unearned and issued to you as a valued member of the CVS/pharmacy ExtraCare program. These coupons take the form of "open ended" coupons such as $3 off $15 or a certain dollar amount off a specific item. In any given transaction our registers will allow only one "open ended" coupon per transaction. CVS Extra Buck coupons are earned when you make a qualifying purchase. These print out instantly at the register upon reaching the threshold for the offer. You can use more than one Extra Buck coupon provided the purchase threshold has been met for each offer on a per-transaction basis.

In the case where a particular item is on sale for "buy one get one free" (BOGO), you are only allowed to use one manufacturer's BOGO coupon. For instance, if Revlon lipstick is on sale for BOGO, you can use one manufacturer's BOGO coupon. You would get both items free and pay any applicable tax. We reserve the right to limit quantities after the first purchase. If our store is running a sale for BOGO, you can use two manufacturer's coupons for a specific dollar amount off. For example, if Revlon lipstick is on sale at our store for BOGO, you can use two $1.00 off Revlon lipstick manufacturer coupons.

CVS/pharmacy does accept manufacturers' coupons that have been obtained from manufacturer sponsored and/or authorized Web sites. The coupon should be complete and contain a bar code that can be scanned at the register. If the coupon does not scan, the cashier should politely inform you that we cannot accept your coupon. We do not allow manual overrides at the register for coupons printed from the Internet. CVS/pharmacy will not accept offers printed from unauthorized Internet postings or reproductions, copies, or facsimiles.

We do not accept competitors' coupons for front store items. We feel that our sales and ExtraCare program are comparable if not better than any sales or coupons offered by our competitors. We also do not accept any expired coupons, CVS or otherwise. We do not "double" or "triple" coupons.

Giant Eagle

The following guidelines apply to all forms of coupons:

The coupon has a valid expiration date and has not expired. Only 1 coupon per item(s) purchased as stated on the coupon with a maximum of 12 coupons per same 12 items purchased.

Coupon value cannot exceed the price of the item(s) purchased. The original coupon must be presented. Photo copies will not be accepted.

Product must be purchased in sizes specified on the coupon. Items must be purchased at the time of redemption. If you forget to use your coupons at the time of purchase, we will accept them with your receipt and Giant Eagle Advantage Card® up to 7 days beyond the date on the receipt.

Additional guidelines apply for the following forms of coupons:

eOffer™ Coupons: Must be obtained from our designated Web site or approved third-party websites (approved third-party sites are listed on gianteagle.com/faq/eoffers).

∘eOffers™ must be clipped and loaded onto your Giant Eagle Advantage Card® prior to redemption.
Are not subject to doubling.

Printed Internet coupons:

The coupon must be obtained from a legitimate site.

We reserve the right to refuse any coupons that we believe to be photo copied, counterfeit or invalid for any other reason. Any coupon with a value over $3 will not be accepted except where advertised by Giant Eagle® for a specific promotion. No "FREE" or "Buy One Get One Free" coupons will be accepted.

Check Out Coupons:

Only coupons that say 'redeemable at Giant Eagle®' will be accepted and are not subject to doubling.

Giant Eagle® coupons must have a Giant Eagle®, GetGo® or Market District® logo on the coupon
and are not subject to doubling.

Double Coupons

We may choose to offer double value up to a stated amount where applicable when the following guidelines are met:

Manufacturers' coupons are doubled only with your Giant Eagle Advantage Card®

Redeem any manufacturer's coupon with a valid expiration date, worth up to and including the stated maximum amount clipped from newspapers, magazines or received by mail and we'll double the savings. Coupons worth more than the stated maximum amount will be redeemed at face value only.

Cigarettes, tobacco and milk or any other items prohibited by law or the manufacturer are excluded.

Policy may change without notice.

Harris Teeter

We accept coupons that have not passed their expiration date for use; we cannot accept any expired coupons.

We accept only one manufacturer coupon per purchased item.

We do not accept coupons on items not purchased.

Coupons must be presented at time of purchase; we cannot return money for coupons not used.

Coupons presented and items purchased must match exactly; size, variety, flavor, etc.

We uphold any purchase stipulations set forth by product manufacturer.

We accept one coupon per item purchased.

We accept coupons for items only of equal or more value; we do not give cash back.

Sales tax is paid by customer at full retail.

Doubling

We accept 20 double coupons per day per customer/household with VIC card; all others redeemed at face value. No orders may be separated that would allow the 20 coupon limit or any other coupon limits to be exceeded. We double manufacturer's coupons up to face value of $0.99; with total amount not to exceed $1.98 or entire retail of item; whichever is less.

We double up to three identical items with manufacturer coupon; additional coupons for like item will be honored at face value. Like items include all flavors.

No competitor coupons will be doubled or tripled. Coupons that state "do not double" should not be doubled or tripled.

eVIC coupons can be accepted along with paper coupons, however will not be doubled.

Internet Coupons

We gladly accept internet manufacturer's coupons for product;
however no "free" product internet coupons are accepted.

With the purchase of two like manufacturer's products, we accept
two internet coupons, per store, per day.
We do not accept internet coupons that do not appear to be
originals or that won't scan.

Competitor's Coupons

We gladly accept local competitors' manufacturer coupons. We
also redeem circular or direct-mail coupons for money off of the
total order.

We do not accept any internet coupons from other retailers.

Rainchecks

Rainchecks never expire and are accepted at any Harris Teeter.

We do not issue rainchecks for coupon items that may be out of
stock or for "while supplies last" items.

We reserve the right to limit raincheck quantities based on product
availability and advertised limits.

Rainchecks can be written for a limit of three unless otherwise
stated in the ad.

Scan Guarantee
Our scan guarantee states "If an item scans higher than the shelf
tag or sign, you will receive one like item free, excluding alcohol
and tobacco."

We will honor five "scan guarantees" per customer; all other
pricing inadequacies will result in the difference between the shelf
tag and the actual price of the item being refunded.

Harris Teeter reserves the right to limit quantities in coupon usage,
as well as products and to amend our policies as we deem
appropriate.

Hyvee

The following rules apply when accepting vendor coupons clipped from newspapers or magazines, received by mail, or obtained legitimately from the internet:

The coupon must be legible.

The coupon should have a scannable bar code (UPC) and a remittable manufacturer's address.

Coupons must have an expiration date and must be used within the stated time frame. Expired coupons will not be accepted.

Only one vendor coupon per item will be accepted. However, a customer may use a vendor coupon in combination with a Hy-Vee coupon on the same item.

Coupon values that exceed the price of the item will not be accepted.

Soft drink container caps will be accepted.

Due to increased fraud, the following two additional rules apply to internet coupons:

Vendor coupons that involve any kind of free product will not be accepted, including "buy one, get one free" offers. A Store Director has authority to set monetary limitations (for example, $2.50 per coupon) for the acceptance of internet coupons.

Kmart

We accept any manufacturer's coupons that have a scannable bar code and that are not copied from an original coupon. Upon using the coupon, it must be surrendered to the cashier.

We accept $5 off coupons, BOGO offer coupons, and free product coupons, but they are not doubled during our double coupon events.

We do accept internet printable coupons as long as they have a scannable bar code. They may be printed in black and white. More than one coupon may not be used on a single product.

During our double coupon events, there is a limit, and that limit varies by event.

Meijer

When accepting coupons, Meijer uses the following guidelines:

We accept two kinds of coupons; Meijer issued coupons and manufacturer coupons.

Only one manufacturer coupon and one Meijer coupon for the same item will be accepted (unless prohibited).

Mealbox coupons are considered Meijer coupons.

We accept all valid internet coupons. See store for details.

We reserve the right to limit quantities.

If the value of the coupon is more than the price of the item after discounts or coupons are applied, the value of the coupon will be applied up to the price of the item.

We do not apply the excess value of a coupon to the order total if the value of the coupon is over the price of the item after discounts or coupons are applied.

Only coupons for products carried in our stores will be accepted.

All coupons should be given to the cashier while you're checking out and cannot be applied to a previous purchase.

To get free in-store coupons, visit: meijermealbox.com

Kroger

All Kroger store divisions accept industry-standard, secure print-at-home coupons.

We can only accept print-at-home coupons if they scan properly at checkout. Legitimate printable coupons are delivered using special software designed to print a properly rendered barcode on the coupon and limit the number of coupons printed.

We will generally not accept "FREE product" (no purchase required) print-at-home coupons. It is currently an industry practice not to produce print-at-home manufacturer's coupons for free product. Buy-one-get-one-free coupons and other values that have a purchase requirement are acceptable.

We will usually not accept coupons for more than above 75% of a product's value. For example, a $2 off coupon will be acceptable for a product that normally sells for $5 or more, but a $2 off printable coupon for a product that sells for $2.25 is unlikely to be legitimate. If there are exceptions, we are usually provided advance notice by the manufacturer.

Coupons will be rejected if they appear distorted or blurry, altered in any way, or are obvious duplicates. You should always print the coupon yourself directly from the website or email that is offering it. Only then can you ensure you are printing a legitimate coupon. The coupon will never appear on your computer screen. A legitimate coupon is never sent as a graphic or PDF or sent in a Word document.

Rewards points can be earned in the following ways:

Spend $100 on groceries, earn 100 points. ($1 = 1 point)

Spend $50 on gift cards and we double the points. (1 $50 gift card = 100 points)

Fill or refill 2 prescriptions at a Kroger Pharmacy. (1 prescription = 50 pts)

Publix

Publix accepts manufacturers' coupons (limit one per item), Publix coupons (originals only—no copies), valid Internet coupons, and coupons from nearby competitors identified by each Publix store. (Competitor names are posted at each Publix store.)

We will accept coupons from competing pharmacies for prescriptions only. We will not accept percent-off-items or percent-off-total-order coupons.

We will only accept coupons for identical merchandise we sell. Acceptance is subject to any restrictions on the coupon, and we reserve the right to limit quantities. Manager approval is needed for individual coupons above $5.00. For a buy-one-get-one free (BOGO) offer, each item is considered a separate sale. We will accept a manufacturer's coupon and either a Publix or a competitor coupon on the same item. Dollars-off-total-order coupons will be limited to one Publix and one competitor coupon per order. The order total must be equal to or greater than the total purchase requirements indicated on the coupon(s) presented.

Rite Aid

Rite Aid will accept internet / print at home coupons up to the equivalent value of $5.00 off.

A Rite Aid coupon (with the Rite Aid logo) is NOT considered an internet coupon (even if printed off the internet) and is therefore not subject to the $5.00 maximum.

+UP Reward Coupons

+UP Reward coupons are special coupons earned by a customer in a prior purchase that can be used for any non-prescription purchase with a small number of exclusions that are listed on the +UP coupon.

Multiple +UP coupons can be used (subject to the printed exclusions) up to the amount of purchase before sales tax.

Buy One, Get One Free

Rite Aid accepts Buy One, Get One Free coupons, however only one coupon can be used for each pair of items purchased. A customer can use one "cents off" coupon in conjunction with the item they are purchasing on a Buy One Get One Free promotion (or with a Buy One Get One Free coupon), although the value of the cents off coupon cannot exceed the selling price of the item. Buy One Get One Free coupons cannot be used in conjunction with a Buy One Get One Free promotion.

Total Purchase Coupons

Rite Aid may feature total purchase coupons which discount the total purchase amount based upon meeting specific requirements. For example, $5 off a $25 purchase price threshold coupon.

These coupons are accepted under the following conditions:

The coupon is valid and in date; only one total purchase coupon per transaction.

Total purchase equals or exceeds $25 before tax (before any coupons are applied).

Coupons for individual items can also be used including another "48" coupon that is tied to an item in the transaction. Provided the total of items purchased is equal to or greater than the purchase requirement, other coupons can be used in conjunction with the total purchase coupon.

General Coupon Guidelines

Coupons must be valid and in date; Coupons cannot be exchanged for cash.

Register will validate coupon through scanning or keyed entry of the coupon UPC number.

In the event that any item's selling price is less than the value of the coupon, Rite Aid will accept the coupon in exchange for the selling price of the item. Coupon redemption can never exceed the selling price of an item and no cash back is allowed. When making a return for a product that had a coupon attached, Rite Aid cannot refund cash for the value of the coupon and cannot return the coupon that was used. Rite Aid reserves the right to not accept any coupon where the validity or the coupon cannot be established.

Multiple Coupons

More than one coupon can be used on the purchase of a single item under the following conditions:
All coupons match the item being purchased.

The total of the coupons is equal to or less than the selling price of the item before sales tax.

No more than one "48" Rite Aid Valuable coupon, one "49" Rite Aid Manufacturer coupon, and one "5" Manufacturer coupon can be used on a single item.

Rite Aid may accept up to 4 identical coupons for the same number of qualifying items as long as there is sufficient stock to satisfy other customers within the store manager's sole discretion.

Safeway

Manufacturer and Store Coupons:

1. We will redeem coupons only for the specific items included in our customer's purchase transaction. The redemption value will be as stated on the coupon, unless that value yields a final price for such item less than zero; if application of the redemption value yields a price less than zero, the coupon will be redeemed only for the amount that yields a zero price (our customer cannot net a cash credit or payout from a coupon purchase).

2. Paper coupons must be presented at the time of the purchase transaction. We will accept only coupons issued by Safeway or the manufacturer of the relevant product. We will not accept photocopies of coupons.

3. Coupons are subject to advertised offer limitations and all other limitations and restrictions on the applicable coupon or product.

4. Coupons may not be applied against any free item received in any offer.

5. Coupons have no cash value.

6. Safeway will not accept manufacturer coupons (including, but not limited to, coupons issued through a Catalina or other in-store coupon dispenser) that display another retailer's logo or name unless such coupon is for a specific item with the same product identifiers as the product included in our customer's purchase transaction.

7. We will not accept coupons unless they have an expiration date. Expired coupons will not be accepted.

8. We will not accept coupons that, in the determination of Safeway personnel, appear distorted or blurry or are altered in any way.

9. Sales taxes will be applied in accordance with the law of the applicable state, regardless of any coupon or other discount that may apply to the purchase transaction.

10. All applicable bottle and packaging deposits on the purchased and free items must be paid by the customer.

11. Safeway reserves the right to refuse any coupons at its discretion.

12. Purchase reward thresholds (if any) will be calculated based upon customer's final price (after deducting Club Card savings and all other discounts and savings) before deductions for any manufacturer coupons. As an example (and not as an offer), if a $10 minimum purchase is required for a customer reward, a customer's order at full retail would be $12, a Club Card discount of $1.75 applies, and a manufacturer's coupon of $1 applies, the customer would be given credit for a $10.25 purchase, and would be eligible for the reward (assuming compliance with all other requirements) even though the customer's cash payment would be only $9.25. The manufacturer's coupon would not be deducted from the total for purposes of determining reward eligibility. Purchase reward thresholds (if any) will be calculated based upon customer's final price (after deducting Club Card savings, and all other discounts)

13. References to a threshold purchase requirement will exclude purchases of: Beer, Wine, Spirits, Tobacco Products, Fuel, All Fluid Items in the Refrigerated Dairy Section (including Fluid Dairy and Dairy Substitutes), Prescription Items and Co-payments, Bus/Commuter Passes, Fishing/Hunting Licenses and Tags, Postage Stamps, Money Orders, Money Transfers, Ski Tickets, Amusement Park Tickets, Event Tickets, Lottery Tickets, Phone Cards, Gift Cards, and Gift Certificates; also excluded are: Bottle Deposits, Redemption Values, and Sales Taxes.

Internet Printed Coupons:

14. We gladly accept internet printed coupons. The same manufacturer and store coupon rules above apply to all internet printed coupons.

15. Internet printed coupons must be capable of scanning at checkout.

16. Internet printed coupons must have serial numbers and must follow an industry-standard format.

17. Manufacturer internet printed coupons must clearly indicate that they are a manufacturer coupon and must have a valid manufacture address on the printed coupon.

18. We will not accept "free product" internet printed manufacturer coupons.

Load to Card Club Coupons:

19. Internet and digital coupons that have been electronically loaded to a Safeway Club Card are automatically redeemed at the time of purchase after the club card number has been entered. All other coupon policies above apply to electronic coupons that are loaded to a club card.

Doubling of Coupons:

20. Check with your local store regarding 'double coupon' advertised promotions where customers will receive double the coupon face value off the regular or club card price up to the advertised limit. Not all locations offer double coupon promotions. Limitations and restrictions for double coupon promotions may change at any time. Changes will be posted in store only.

Coupon Stacking:

21. Safeway does not allow a customer to redeem two or more manufacturer coupons against the same item in a single transaction.

22. Coupon stacking policies for manufacturer coupons apply to paper and electronic coupons that have been loaded to a club card.

23. If a customer presents two coupons for the same item in a single transaction, Safeway will give the highest discount for that item, subject to the terms of the applicable offer and/or coupon.

Stop & Shop

Our policy for redeeming manufacturers' coupon is as follows:

Only 1 manufacturers' coupon may be redeemed per item; No substitutions are allowed.

The exact item stated on the coupon be must be purchased in order to redeem the coupon.

Coupons cannot be redeemed after the expiration date stated on the coupon. The total redemption value of the coupon may not exceed the retail value of the item purchased.

Any coupons for "free" products will be honored for the value of the item only. "Free" coupons cannot be doubled or tripled.

Act Media coupons cannot be doubled or tripled.

Product specific Checkout Coupons cannot be doubled or tripled.

Product specific Checkout Coupons cannot be used with any other manufacturers' coupons for the same item.

Non-product specific store Checkout Coupons can be used with another manufacturers' coupon. For example: a customer my use a coupon for "50¢ off any Produce item" and a manufacturers' coupon on the same item.

Double Coupons

We double the savings marked on manufacturers' cents-off coupons up to 99¢. Any coupon $1 and over will be redeemed at face value of the item purchased. In cases where the double coupon total exceeds the value of the item, the offer is limited to the retail price. Lottery tickets, cigarettes, tax and items prohibited by law are excluded.

You may double a maximum of 4 identical manufacturers' coupons. For example: if a customer purchased five boxes of Cheerios and presented 5 manufacturers' coupons for 50¢, the first four coupons would be doubled to $1. The fifth coupon would only be redeemed for 50¢.

Up to an additional 12 identical manufacturers' coupons/items will be redeemed at face value for a total of 16 identical manufacturers' coupons.

Stop & Shop does not accept competitor's coupons.

We do accept Internet coupons unless we are notified of fraudulent activity involving specific Internet coupons.

Target

Target accepts one manufacturer coupon and one Target coupon for the same item (unless wording on the coupon says otherwise).

Super Target coupons can be used in any Target store if the store carries the item.

Target gladly accepts valid internet coupons.

Coupon amount may be reduced if it exceeds the value of the item after other discounts or coupons are applied.

Price Matching

A guest can use coupons when price matching per Target's normal coupon policy. When the guests presents a coupon(s), these steps will be followed:

Manufacturer Coupons:

Manufacturer coupons will be applied after the price match is made.

Target Coupons:

Target coupons will be applied before the price match is made. If the competitor price is still lower than the price after the Target coupon has been deducted, the ad match can be adjusted to match the competitor's price.

Combining both a Target and Manufacturer Coupons:
The Target coupon will be applied before the price match is made. If the competitor price is still lower than the price after the Target coupon has been deducted, the ad match can be adjusted to match the competitor's price. Once the price match is made the manufacturer coupon will be applied.

Reminder: We accept one manufacturer coupon and one Target coupon for the same item unless either coupon prohibits it.

Walgreens

As a customer-focused retailer, Walgreens encourages the use of coupons by our customers in our retail stores, in accordance with the following guidelines.

All valid coupons should be presented to the cashier at the time of checkout.

Walgreens does not accept expired coupons.

Coupons cannot be exchanged for cash or gift cards.

Competitor coupons are not accepted at Walgreens.

Walgreens cannot accept coupons for items not carried in our store locations.

The number of manufacturer coupons, including Register Rewards manufacturer coupons, may not exceed the number of items in the transaction. The total value of the coupons may not exceed the value of the transaction. Sales tax must be paid, if required by law.

Any coupon offer not covered in these guidelines will be accepted at the discretion of Walgreens management.

Sale Items

Walgreens will accept coupons for an item that is on sale.

In the event that any item's selling price is less than the value of the coupon, Walgreens will only accept the coupon in exchange for the selling price of the item. Coupon redemption can never exceed the selling price of an item and no cash back is ever provided in exchange for any coupons.

Multiple Coupons

When purchasing a single item, Walgreens accepts one manufacturer coupon and applicable Walgreens coupon(s) for the purchase of a single item, unless prohibited by either coupon offer.

The coupon amount must be reduced if it exceeds the value of the item after other discounts or coupons are applied. (For example, a $5.00 coupon for a $4.99 item will result in a $4.99 coupon value).

When purchasing multiple items, Walgreens accepts multiple identical coupons for multiple qualifying items as long as there is sufficient stock to satisfy other customers.

Walgreens Store Management reserves the right to limit the quantity of items purchased.

Buy One, Get One Free Coupons

When items are featured in a Buy One, Get One Free promotion, up to two coupons can be used against the items being purchased, as long as the net price does not go below zero for the items being purchased.

Sales tax must be paid for any Buy One, Get One Free coupon offers, if required by applicable state laws.

Internet/Print at Home Coupons

Walgreens accepts valid internet/print at home coupons.

Register Rewards coupons

Earning Register Rewards

Register Rewards will only print for in-stock merchandise during the promotional period.
Register Rewards can only be earned for eligible items.

No substitutions.

There is a limit of one Register Rewards printed per offer per customer per transaction.

Customers redeeming a Register Rewards against the same offer may not receive another RR.

Redeeming Register Rewards

The RR coupon value cannot exceed the total purchase amount.
No cash back and no cash value for RR coupon.

The number of manufacturer coupons, including RR manufacturer coupons, must not exceed the number of items in the transaction.

Register Rewards must be forfeited if the qualifying merchandise is returned.

Register Rewards cannot be used toward the purchase of gift cards and pre-paid cards.

Register RewardsTM can be redeemed for eligible items only. Ineligible items include but are not limited to:

Prescriptions
Tobacco products
Alcoholic beverages
Dairy products
Lottery tickets
Money orders/transfers
Transportation passes
Special event/entertainment tickets or passes

Postage stamps
Prescription Savings Club" memberships
Health care services, including immunizations
Any items prohibited by law

About Balance Rewards Points:

When purchasing items and/or services at a Participating Store,
Member may choose to either redeem earned Points or continue
saving Points to use on a future purchase of items and/or services.
If Member elects to redeem earned Points, the Points will be
converted into Redemption Dollars and the value of the
Redemption Dollars will be deducted from the total price of the
Member's purchase of items and/or services from a Participating
Store. Earned Points are converted into Redemption Dollars in
eight (8) tiers:

(1) 1,000 points = $1
(2) 2,000 points = $2
(3) 3,000 points = $3
(4) 5,000 points = $5
(5) 10,000 points = $10
(6) 18,000 points = $20
(7) 30,000 points = $35
(8) 40,000 points = $50

Redemption Dollars will not be paid out in cash or Store Credit.

Redemption Dollars may not be used for the purchase of the
following: dairy; alcohol; tobacco; stamps; phone/pre-paid/gift
cards; money order/transfers; transportation passes;
charitable donations; prescriptions; pseudoephedrine or ephedrine
products;immunizations, health tests or other healthcare items or
services; Prescription Savings Club membership fee; clinic
services.

Upon redemption of Points,the Points will immediately be
deducted from Member's account. Once Points are redeemed,
Points cannot be credited back to Member's account. When
returning items paid with Redemption Dollars, the Redemption
Dollars will be refunded to Member in the form of store credit. The
sale or barter of Points, or any other award or benefit (other than
by the Company) is expressly prohibited. Any Points, award, or

benefit transferred, assigned, or sold in violation of the terms and conditions will be confiscated and membership in the Program may be terminated.

Should any Balance Rewards Member not use their card (physical card, virtual card via smartphone or phone number look-up) in a transaction for 6 consecutive calendar months, the membership will be deemed to be inactive and all accumulated Points will be forfeited. For active Members, all Balance Rewards Points expire on a rolling 36-month basis. Complete terms and conditions of Point redemption are posted at Walgreens.com

Walmart

Walmart gladly accepts the following types of coupons:

Print-at-home internet coupons:

Must be legible

Must have "Manufacturer Coupon" printed on them

Must have a valid remit address for the manufacturer

Must have a valid expiration date

Must have a scannable bar code

Buy one, get one free (BOGO) coupons with a specified price. Are acceptable in black and white or color May not be duplicated

Manufacturers' coupons

For dollar/cents off

For free items (except those printed off the Internet) Buy one, get one free (BOGO) coupons Must have "Manufacturer Coupon" printed on them

Must have a valid remit address for the manufacturer

Must have a valid expiration date

Must have a scannable bar code

May not be duplicated

Competitors' coupons

A specific item for a specified price, for example, $2.99

Buy one, get one free coupons for items with a specified price.

Must have "Manufacturer Coupon" with specific item requirements printed on them

Must have a valid remit address for the manufacturer

Must have a valid expiration date

Must have a scannable bar code

Are acceptable in black and white
May not be duplicated

We DO NOT accept the following coupons:

Dollars/cents off the entire basket purchase. Percentage off the entire basket purchase.

Print-at-home Internet coupons that require no purchase.

Double or triple-value coupons.

The following are guidelines and limitations:

Coupons must be presented at the time of purchase.
Only one coupon per item.

Item purchased must be identical to the coupon (size, quantity, brand, flavor, color, etc).

There is no limit on the number of coupons per transaction.

Coupons must have an expiration date and be redeemed prior to expiration. **If coupon value exceeds the price of the item, the**

excess may be given to the customer as cash or applied toward the basket purchase.

SNAP items purchased in a SNAP transaction are ineligible for cash back.

WIC items purchased in a WIC transaction are applied to the basket purchase and may not be eligible for cash back. Refer to state-specific WIC guidelines.

Great Value, Marketside, Equate, Parents Choice, and World Table coupons have no cash value and are ineligible for cash back or application to the basket purchase.

The system will prompt for supervisor verification for:

40 coupons per transaction.

A coupon of $20 or greater on one item.

$50 or more in coupons in one transaction.

Whole Foods

Whole Foods accepts the following types of coupons:

Vendor coupons (provided that they are not intended or labeled for use at another establishment),

Whole Foods Market store coupons,

Coupons may be printed at home in color or black and white as long as they are intended for home printing,

Coupons may be combined with sales and all other store discounts,

Whole Foods Market does not limit the number of coupons per transaction provided that the number of coupons does not exceed the number of products,

Coupons may be combined or "stacked" on one item as long as the combination is one vendor and one store coupon. More than one of the same coupons may never be used on one items.

The following coupons or procedures will not be accepted:

Photocopied or duplicated coupons,
Doubled or tripled coupons,
Altered or expired coupons,

Coupons that are not completely intact including missing expiration date or barcode.

Whole Foods Market does not match competitor prices or take competitor coupons.

If a product is BOGO and therefore free, a coupon may not be used for its purchase.

If the value of the coupon exceeds the value of the product the value of the coupon will be altered by the difference. No overages or cash back on coupons will be allowed.

Team or store leadership reserves the right to refuse a coupon if its authenticity cannot be validated.